TEACH ME TIGER!

MY AUTOBIOGRAPHY

Copyright © 2013 April Stevens
All rights reserved.
ISBN: 1490434658
ISBN 13: 9781490434650

I dedicate this book to my mother and father, for without their effort and sacrifices, my brother, Nino, and I would never have achieved the successes we did.

Contents

1	The Early Years	1
2	Sam and Anna	9
3	Carol and Nino	15
4	California	23
5	April Stevens	31
6	Glenn McCarthy	43
7	Back to the Shamrock	53
8	Learning to Drive	63
9	Cary Grant	65
10	Teach Me Tiger	69
11	Deep Purple	73
12	Grammy Awards	83
13	Traveling	85
14	Righteous Brothers	117
15	The Seventies	121
16	Home in Los Angeles	125
17	Dad	127
18	Bill	129
19	The Wedding	141
20	Africa	153
21	Pinetop	159
22	Buffalo Music Hall of Fame	161
23	The Present	163

Epilogue	165
Mom's Recipes	167
Letters from Servicemen	173
Discography Single Releases	185

Acknowledgements

This book would not have been written if it hadn't been for the encouragement of my dear friend Susan Alexander. She introduced me to the talented John Sullivan, and he showed me the way, "literally." Susan then brought me Nancy Hellner, who painstakingly unscrambled my scribbling and typed for hours on end. To Sandra Potts for her kindness in helping me at the beginning. Also to Jean Van Epps for her wonderful skills finishing the final draft. Thanks to Jim Chaffin, who consistently came to my rescue with the answers to my many questions. To my brother, Nino Tempo, for sharing all of our adventures and remembering details that I didn't. And last but not least, my gratitude to my loving husband, Bill, for his patience and coming to my aid at the end of my story and for his careful editing and help in the final publishing. It wasn't easy!

Foreword

Honor Thy Gift
I had so much more to give.
I just scratched the surface.
I fell in love and turned my back on
a God-given gift.
That is what hurts my heart the most.

But in spite of the wrong choices I made, I thank God.
I have been so very lucky all my life.

With love,

April

Prologue

Did Steve Allen just announce our names and *Deep Purple* as the Best Rock and Roll Record of the year? Or am I hearing things? It was May 12, 1964, and my brother, Nino, and I were at our first Grammy Award dinner at the Beverly Hilton Hotel in Beverly Hills. My mouth was full of the food I was chewing, and I thought my hearing was impaired. But the look on Nino's face said it all. His eyes were glazed over, and he was staring at one spot, kind of bewildered looking. He stood up and moved toward the stage in a daze, and I followed, gulping my food down. The applause was so loud! The audience was so happy for us! How did this happen? How did we get here?

CHAPTER 1

The Early Years

Wasn't the whole world Italian? That's what I believed as a child growing up in Niagara Falls, New York. Everyone had dark eyes and hair and looked like me. All the older folks spoke with a similar accent, and we all ate the same food. Pasta and meatballs, con *sardi* with olive oil and anchovies, chicken Sicilian wedding soup with tiny meatballs, and plenty of salads.

It wasn't until the end of kindergarten and the beginning of the first grade that I began to realize that there were other nationalities. I met people of color and people with blond or red hair and blue or green eyes. That is when my fascination with light eyes began. A girl in my first grade class named Patty Ann had beautiful pale blue eyes with black-fringed lashes, and I could not take my eyes off of her eyes! I don't believe I have ever had an attraction to or a relationship with a man who did not have blue or green eyes. (My husband, Bill, has outstanding green eyes, and they look blue when he wears blue.)

My parents were Sam and Anna LoTempio. Their parents emigrated from Sicily in the late 1800s and landed at Ellis Island in New York City. What a journey, and how very fearless and courageous they were, going on hearsay and hope as to what they would find in America.

We are full-blooded Sicilians. My father's parents came over first from a small village called Valledolmo near Palermo, Sicily. My grandfather was Antonino LoTempio, born in August 1859. My grandmother was Vincinette (Vincenza in Italian) Gugino, born in 1866. They were both from the same small village. They settled in Buffalo and then later in Niagara Falls. I don't know very much about them, and there are few people left to ask who might know details.

My dad's parents were at least twenty years older than my mom's parents, and my dad was the last of six children, four boys and two girls. One sister, Caroline, died before I was born. I was named after her. My dad's other sister was Theresa, and she was very dear to me.

My grandmother passed away before I was born, and my grandfather remarried and died shortly after I was born. He said, "Carolina was born a little too late for me."

My grandfather owned a very large grocery import store in an area where many black people lived. He had all of the good food from the old country—the olives, cheeses, cold cuts, boxes of the different pastas, and the best wines. They were considered wealthy by the standard of those days.

I remember when I was about five or six years old, we were visiting my Aunt Theresa's house, close to where the big grocery store was, and it seemed so huge and still so empty. I asked my dad on the way home if we could stop and listen to the singing at the black revival church. He said "maybe," and that would always hold me because "no" was so final.

I would stand outside the door and take in the beautiful, thrilling voices that would actually fill the air. I remember saying, "Daddy, isn't it so special?" Even then, it was such a treat to my ears.

Mom told me that when my grandfather died in 1930, he left his money divided equally among his five living children.

But my dad didn't get his share of his parents' inheritance, and it was a considerable amount. I don't know what happened. It was a mystery—to me, anyway.

My grandfather was very well known in Niagara Falls, and he was very influential because of his prosperous business. He was a smart, capable man. I always remember Mom saying he was so sweet and quite an unusual man. I wish I could have known him.

On my mother's side, my grandmother's birth name was Vita Cardone. She was born in a province of Messina, Sicily, called Condro, on February 2, 1890. My grandfather, Bartalomeo Donia, was born in the same small town of Condro on March 29, 1884. My grandmother came to this country and settled in Punxsutawney, Pennsylvania, with her father, mother, and two brothers. My grandfather came to the Land of Opportunity around the same time. My grandfather had heard about the Cardones also coming from Condro, and thought he would look them up, although they did not know each other.

Yes, my maternal grandparents met in Punxsutawney, Pennsylvania, where my grandmother's family owned a boarding house. Punxsutawney is a Native American name, and the city is known for its celebration of Groundhog Day every February 2. Like many others in those days, my grandfather worked in the coal mines there—not a very healthful job but profitable and steady. My grandfather needed to rent a room.

The story, as Mom told it (and she was usually right), is that when my grandparents met at the boarding house and looked at each other, they fell madly in love. He was so handsome and manly looking, and she looked like Loretta Young, the beautiful actress. Is it any wonder?

I always questioned what my mom said, saying, "Impossible! You can't fall in love that easily. You must really know the person." She stuck to her story, and I found out years later that she was right. Love at first sight can happen. It happened to me when I met my husband. I knew instantly that at long last, he was the one. I'll tell you about it later.

In Italy, the word for grandmother was *nonna*, and the word for grandfather was *nonno*. My grandparents didn't know each other in the old country, which was strange since the town of Condro's population is only five hundred, even today. But my nonno was six years older than she was, and their ages may have been the reason they did not run into each other.

After a brief time, they were married in 1906. My nonna was sixteen years old and my nonno was twenty-two, and they were together all of their lives. My nonna never faltered in her love for him. He came before all of their daughters; he was number one. She was so in love with him. My nonno liked the ladies, but she was his true love.

Mom was the firstborn in 1907 in Punxsutawney. When she was eighteen months old, my grandparents heard that Italy was putting an army together. There was some unrest, and my grandfather thought he had to join the Italian Army. Can you imagine? So they packed up my mom and took a boat back to Italy. They later learned that my grandfather didn't have to join the army in Italy if he lived in America! What a trip that must have been! Going all that way with an eighteen-month-old baby when it wasn't necessary. How they must have laughed—or cried.

They remained in Sicily for two years, weathering a devastating eruption from Mt. Etna and saving enough money for their trip back. My mom learned to speak Italian very quickly. She didn't remember very many things except walking barefoot on the lovely tile floors. For years afterward, whenever she walked on tile barefoot, that memory kicked in.

After a short while, they were back in Pennsylvania, but they soon moved to Highland Avenue in Niagara Falls, New York.

They picked that city because it was an up-and-coming, moneymaking community. My grandfather needed money because he had plans for many children. He wanted a boy so badly, and every time it was a girl—again—my grandmother cried, and he would smile and reassure her with, "That's just what I wanted."

All of their daughters except Mom were born on Highland Avenue. My grandfather bought a bar, Bart's Bar, close to the house. It was successful with a mostly Irish and Italian clientele. A sign up on the bar read, "We do not serve drink to Indians and Irishmen." That gave everyone a good laugh. He had hardboiled eggs and pigs' feet on the bar for the customers to eat, and he was known for singing all the Irish songs with a thick Italian accent. He was quite a character and very much liked and admired. People learned that he could be trusted and was a man of his word. He did well.

One of his daughters, Sarah, next to Mom in age, used to help him sling beer when he got too busy. She must have been fifteen or so and was a strong and happy girl. Today she is 103 years old.

There were so many people of different nationalities settling in the area: Polish, Italian, and Irish, with all the different dialects. I truly don't know how they all ever understood each other, but the strange thing is, they did. They managed to figure it all out and become friends. Amazing!

Niagara seasons were quite extreme. The summers were hot and the winters were cold, but the fall with all the colored falling leaves and the temperate spring made up for it; they were so pretty. And then, of course, there was the attraction of the breathtaking Niagara Falls. What a thrill that is to see. People flocked there with money to spend.

They moved again in 1924. My grandfather bought an apartment building on the corner of Fifteenth Street and Pine Avenue in the center of town. It had nine apartments on two floors with a restaurant and small bar attached to the building. Directly on the corner was a small A&P grocery store. He bought it all for twenty thousand dollars. He then bought a house directly in the back of the property and built a garage for his car.

He and my grandmother, Vita, owned the Pine Avenue Rainbow Grill. I was always so happy to go there. It was only two blocks away from where we lived. Half of it was a saloon, and the other half was a small restaurant with about six tables. It had a very tiny kitchen where my nonna cooked her delicious Sicilian specialties. I don't know how she was even able to cook in that small space. My favorite was spaghetti and meatballs; it still is.

I am so sorry I didn't learn to speak Italian. Instead, my poor nonna had to try to speak English. I can still hear her saying to me in her broken English, "Carolina, have some more meatballs." And as always, I never turned any food down, especially hers.

When I was about seven or eight, I sat at the back table near the kitchen, where we all sat to eat in my grandparents' saloon. I would look toward the bar, and I was fascinated. I could see my nonno with his arms resting on the bar, laughing or singing with the customers. I'd watch pretty ladies come in, and then after three or four hours of drinking and carrying on, I'd see them walk out with a man, disheveled looking and not nearly as lovely. Once, I saw a lady go into the ladies room and a man follow her in. I thought, *He went into the wrong room!* Soon, they both came out, looking extremely disheveled. I learned a lesson that has been with me all my life. I decided that when I grew up and had dates, I would try not to drink more than one glass of alcohol with a man; otherwise, I might mess up and say something I shouldn't or do something I would regret.

Even at that age, I was concerned with how completely different a woman looked going into a bar than when leaving.

Luckily, I don't drink. I don't like the taste of alcohol, and if I have one drink, I really feel it. I'm what you call a cheap drunk!

My nonna would sometimes look out of the large window in the front of the restaurant and watch all of the people go by. It was a very busy, prosperous street in the heart of the city, and if she ever saw servicemen going by, she would step out and offer them some free food. They naturally never said no, and she loved cooking for them.

Because he had a bar again, my nonno was exposed to the public, and he made many new friends. He knew many of the men in the Mafia. As a child, I would ask my mother or my nonna, "What is a Mafia?" They would put their fingers up to their mouths and say, "Shush, don't say that word." It seemed very strange. I would walk away with my finger on my lips, saying, "Shush," mimicking them. It was the same every time I asked them. Finally, I figured it out. It was not to be mentioned.

We lived in an area with Mafia families. They were at school, at church—everywhere. We were all friends, and I never felt a difference. Times were very difficult in the thirties with the Depression, and there was very little money to go around. My mom once told me that a Mafia friend of my grandfather's went to see him at the bar to try to get money for protection, but my grandfather didn't have any extra money. He could barely make ends meet with the large family he had. Although he had an apartment building, a bar, and a restaurant, people were unable to pay him because of hard times. My grandfather even tried bootlegging to make extra money. After much thought, he decided to go to see the head of the Mafia—the Don himself. He brought his books along, and as he sat across from the Don, he said, "Look over my books, and if you can find a way that I can pay you for protection, I will." The Don looked at him and then looked over the books, and after a few minutes, he handed my grandfather the books and said, "Bart, go home and take care of your family."

When I found out about my nonno being part of a bank robbery in Canada, to say I was surprised would be an understatement. I was absolutely dumbfounded. How could it be? How could he have been a part of it? I had no idea for all those years because the family kept it from me. After I got married, one of my aunts must have had too much to drink at one of our dinner parties and told my husband, Bill, the infamous story. He told me what she said, and I couldn't believe it. I immediately asked mom, and she confirmed it and said they had all been too embarrassed to tell me—even years later. Not a word was ever spoken to me about it.

Because of money problems during the Depression, people were doing all kinds of crazy things, and from what I understand, somehow my grandfather and his brother, who had come over from Sicily, became involved with a robbery in Canada in the 1930s. He and his brother were driving the getaway cars. Due to a misunderstanding, they didn't get arrested because they were waiting on the wrong corner! (How lucky can you get?) But they had to go into hiding in Niagara Falls until they were exonerated. However, they were never allowed to set foot in Canada again. At this point in the story, I was laughing hysterically. What else could I do? It was so long ago—but what a shock.

CHAPTER 2

Sam and Anna

My father was born in Buffalo on May 6, 1908, the youngest of six children. Shortly after his mother passed away, his father remarried. He was not fond of his stepmother, but his oldest sister, Theresa, adored him and kept a good eye on him. He worked hard cleaning his brother Charlie's drugstore and his brother Frank's grocery store. He was about twelve or thirteen at the time.

My dad, Sam, was a lovely, gentle man. He was very sweet and quiet, but he could be funny too. I loved him with all of my heart. He was handsome in a Robert De Niro way; he was stockier, but he had the same kind of features. Dad was very musical but shy. He could sing and loved to dance. At a party, all of my mom's sisters wanted to dance with him because of his natural rhythm and because of the way he would hold and lead them on the dance floor. They said he was so suave and cool and light on his feet, and he was so happy to have so many dancing partners.

That's where mom and dad met—at a dance. He was singing and dancing to "Ja-Da (Ja Da, Ja Da, Jing, Jing, Jing!)" It was a popular song back then. He was really getting into it. I always thought he was so shy, but I guess dancing was his thing. And it certainly got Mom's eyes on him—forever. He must have been fifteen or sixteen at that dance because in 1926, when he was eighteen, they were married. Mom was nineteen. She and my dad could not date. All they could do was sit on the front porch with a chaperone. Someone was always with them. Being the first daughter was very hard on her as far as leniency with her parents; they were very strict.

She picked out a beautiful gown that was made in France. She looked stunning on her wedding day. I wore the same dress for my wedding, but that comes later. They went to New York City for their honeymoon. My god, they barely knew each other! When they returned, they moved into a small two-bedroom apartment on Pine Avenue.

My dad was a saver, and when we were young, he taught us to save, even a small amount, whenever money came in. Because of his cautious ways, he was able to open a small grocery store with his nephew, Ned LoTempio, a few years before we left for Los Angeles, California. In 1937, Dad rented the small grocery store attached to my grandfather's property on Fifteenth and Pine Avenue. He and Ned were the owners of the new L&L Food Store.

It was very successful, and the people in the neighborhood loved him because he remembered their names and always had a smile on his face. He was my hero.

My mother was also my hero. She took such good care of us. A very dear friend of mine, Halayne Kasoff, once told me, "Stay close to your mother, April. You will never have a friend like her. No one will ever love you as she does." She was so right. I can never thank her enough for telling me that. Mom loved to shop (but only for sales), so I took her shopping and to lunch often, and it was so much fun! Sometimes we have to be reminded, I'm sorry to say, and my dear friend Halayne always gave me the best advice. I love her for it.

My mom was something else. She was a spitfire when she needed to be but was the sweetest, softest, warmest lady you would ever want to meet. And what a beauty she was! So many men in Niagara Falls wanted to marry her. Even the family doctor waited years for her until she was of age. When she was seventeen, he asked for her hand. But of all of those men, she chose Dad—and he was the proudest man in the world.

My brother, Nino, once asked Dad how he got the courage to get married at eighteen. Dad answered, "You should have seen your mother when I married her." Then he just closed his eyes and shook his head as if to say, "Wow. What a beauty."

Everyone loved Mom. She was friendly, warm, and funny; it all just seemed to jump out of her. When we went shopping and to lunch, I would tell her ahead of time, "Please, Mom, don't talk to everyone. Promise me." But there she was, talking to everyone, her mouth going a mile a minute. And she was always so animated!

I always wondered how she became so smart. She had very little schooling because she had to stay at home and help her mother with all of the babies that kept coming. My grandmother had to cook for the restaurant, and she waitressed there, too. Mom's six sisters were Sarah, three years younger, then Isabel, Frances, Donadell, Antoinette, and finally, my aunt Elaine. I don't remember ever seeing any of my aunts in the restaurant helping my nonna cook. Come to think of it, the kitchen was too small to fit two people.

My mother had such wisdom and intuition. She was almost always right about everything. She knew without a doubt that my brother, Nino, and I had talent, and she was confident enough to help us pursue our dreams when no one in the family, except Dad, believed we could do it. Mom must have heard something in the sound of my singing voice that she determined was so rare and different that it compelled her finally to get Nino and me out of Niagara Falls and into Los Angeles. She left her family and her home to prove that she was right, and she was. If I hadn't messed things up with Glenn McCarthy, I know I could have gone all the way to the top; actually, I was there. I will tell you more about Glenn McCarthy in a later chapter.

Mom was born Anna Donia in 1907, the oldest of seven daughters. My mom said she cried whenever she saw that her mother was pregnant again since she had to help with the new baby's care. It happened six times.

Mom was really very beautiful with long, straight, blue-black hair. She was very fair with dark brown eyes and the most delicate of lovely features. People always stared at her and asked if she was Irish. In 1921, she was sixteen years old. She entered a beauty contest, the Miss America Contest in Niagara Falls, New York. She was by far the most beautiful contestant. She would have won had it not been for one of the other contestant's uncle being one of the judges. The winner went on to the first Miss America Contest in Buffalo. It was all over town that the contest had been unfair.

During that same time, someone sent my mom's photo overseas to the Aly Khan. He was a very powerful man in the Middle East, and he sent an immediate reply stating his desire to meet her. But since her father, Bart Donia, was a typical old-fashioned, strict, Italian father, the answer was a thundering no! He knew exactly what was on the man's mind, and being from the old country, he was tough. His daughters did not have an easy road—my mom especially since she was the firstborn.

I have heard that when Mom about eighteen years old, she went for a walk with her sister Elaine, who must have been three or four years old. My dad met them somewhere along the way, so they tell me, and Mom introduced him to Elaine as Mary. She knew her mother would ask Elaine if anyone else walked with them, and she was right in thinking so. So when her mother asked Elaine the question, she answered, "Yes, Mary walked with us." So Dad was called "Mary" for years by Elaine. Dad must have loved that.

Since Dad didn't get his inheritance, when he first married Mom, he worked two jobs. He was a chauffeur and then a guard at night at a speakeasy during prohibition. That is when the Mafia showed interest in him. He was young, handsome, and streetwise and came from a good family, and they knew he could take care of himself if a situation arose. But his father made it clear to them that my dad would have no part in their organization. He would have made considerable money, but it wasn't worth it. They would have owned him for the rest of his life.

CHAPTER 3

Carol and Nino

I was born Caroline Vincinette LoTempio on April 29, 1929. There, I said it—but everyone called me Carol. How I would run to my dad when he came home from work. He taught me so many things, and he always said, "Be a good girl." I loved to sing. Mom often said that when I was three or four, she would find me in the middle of a group of people, singing my heart out even though I had a definite lisp. I couldn't pronounce my Ss or my Rs. That must have been quite an earful and an eyeful with my tongue flopping around. I'm happy to say that, gradually, my speech did improve, but I grew much shyer, and people were always amazed that I continued to want a singing career. But what else could I possibly do? I thought briefly about nursing because I love people, but the sight of blood was a problem, and singing was so easy for me.

    Now that I have grandchildren, I know how lucky I was and how difficult a task it can be to try to decide what you want to do for the rest of your life.

    On January 6, 1935, when I was almost six years old, my brother, Anthony, or Antonino Bart LoTempio, was born. He was named after my mom's father, Bart, and my father's father, Antonino. We called him Nino. Throughout our career, I always said he was older than I was; I thought that sounded better and made better sense. As the years went by, I almost began to believe it. However, I am older—damn it!

I was crazy about him from the beginning. I was certain I heard the stork flying him to our apartment when he was born! When we were growing up together, I loved taking care of him. I wouldn't let any babysitter take care of him; I sent them home, and I would do it. He was a beautiful baby with Mom's pretty features. He was also very talented and smart.

Music was important in our household, so it was only natural that Nino and I would choose to entertain. But how could we possibly find the road to fame in Niagara Falls, New York?

We would sing together at the foot of the outside stairs at the apartment when he was two and I was eight. We sang "Bye, Bye, Blackbird" and "Show Me the Way to Go Home." They were sentimental songs, and we responded very emotionally to music even at that tender age. One of the songs was named "The Old Apple Tree" and contained the line, "It reminds me of my pappy; he was handsome, young and happy, when he died on the old apple tree." Wow, that line did us in! Tears and laughter at the same time. That is the youngest I remember us singing together.

Quite often, we could all go to Nonna's restaurant, and the four of us would have something special to eat that my nonna had cooked. After dinner, the music on the radio would play and Dad would get up and do his special little dance. He would snap his fingers to the rhythm, hunch his back, and move around the room.

When I was about seven, I would get right behind him and mimic what he did with the exact same rhythm. Then, as soon as Nino could walk, he railed right behind me, doing the exact same dance, not missing a beat, and we would go around the restaurant to the music. Everyone laughed and loved it. What fun it was to see and to do.

We hated to get up in the morning for school because it was so cold and gloomy. In fact, we couldn't get up! Mom had so many blankets on us as we huddled in our twin beds. The Seventeenth Street Grade School was a long block away, and did she ever pile the clothes on us to keep us warm. Poor Nino couldn't even see his feet, so he always seemed to get his rubbers on the wrong foot. You couldn't tell which way he was going. He was so funny.

Mom and Dad seldom left us with a babysitter when we were young. I was afraid of the dark because when I was very young, four or five, I saw a Bela Lugosi movie that really had an effect on me. (Bela Lugosi played Dracula in the early vampire movies.) My poor dad had to sleep on a chair in my bedroom for a week and then get up and go to work the next morning. I didn't seem to outgrow the fear, either.

When I was about nine and Nino was four, Mom and Dad thought it was time to leave us alone for about two hours. I sat still on a chair next to the radio the whole two hours. I didn't move an inch, listening to stories and music. What I was really doing was watching the clock for the two hours to be up and my mom and dad to come home.

Nino was just busy running around the apartment and playing with his new flashlight. I was so mad because he had me to protect him, and I had no one. All of a sudden, he screamed and ran to me and jumped on my lap. As he held me tight he screamed, "Someone's under the bed!" That damn flashlight! I was petrified and shaking with him on my lap. Mom and Dad came in just at that moment. What great timing. Another minute and I think we would have passed out. They showed us that there was nothing under the bed, and what a relief that was. I still like the door ajar when I sleep, I don't like to be alone at night, and I still look under the bed. God help me if I ever find anything!

Nino and I teased, arm wrestled, and fought each other, but there was no greater love. Even though at the beginning I was bigger than he was, he made such strange and funny faces when he was mad that I became weak with laughter, so he would ultimately win.

My first true love was the first Tarzan in the movies, Buster Crabbe. When I was four or five, I came home from school all excited and lisped, "Mommy, tonight can we go to the movies to see Tarzan?" I asked her if he was real, and when she said no, my heart was broken. I remember that day so well. I ran to my room and cried my eyes out. She came running after me, explaining that he was a real person: he was just not really Tarzan. That was OK—as long as he was alive and I could love him.

Nino and I would often walk from our apartment to my grandparents' house on Fifteenth and Pine Avenue. He was so cute. He would walk a few steps behind me and clench his fists at boys that whistled at me as we walked by. He started to protect me even then, and it never stopped. I have been very lucky my whole life, and I'm very aware of it.

When I was eight or nine years old, I was with a girlfriend. We took a shortcut, and I noticed a garage door with a four-letter word scribbled on it. It was a word I had noticed before written on a brick wall with chalk. "What is that word," I asked, "and what does it mean?" My friend told me what she knew, and I was absolutely stunned. I had never heard of such a thing. I just stood there, immobilized. I can't tell you how awful and vile it was to me. It made such an impression on me that I cried every night in my bed, thinking about my parents and how I was born. I'm sure it has happened to many children, and of course, I got over it, but it was a bad time when it happened.

When I was eleven years old, and we had just moved into the new apartment in Niagara Falls, we bought an upright piano. I wanted to take lessons, but only if Nino promised to stay in the room while the teacher taught me because I knew nothing about reading music. Nino had already been taking clarinet lessons, and I couldn't have done it without him. Not that I really did it. Finally, exasperated, the teacher had me read the notes on the music sheet and with a pencil write the notes on each white piano key, so I would know where to put my fingers. I guess he knew I wasn't going very far as a piano player. Finally, I managed to play the one song I learned and memorized, "Dark Eyes." I must have played it one thousand times. I hate that song now!

If we went visiting friends, Mom would say, "Carol, why don't you play the piano for them?" The trouble was that if I made a mistake (and I usually did), I had to go back to the beginning of the song because I lost my place. It took forever to play that damn song! A musical wizard I was not!

Nino and I didn't really think alike. I was the forever optimist who saw the glass half full. Everything was gray, not black and white as it was for him. He is a deep thinker. I am more passive. How often I have heard him say to me, "Are you sure we're related?"

However, in one instance, we were the same. We were taught that integrity was *the* word and that our word was our bond above all! I feel guilty, even today, if I say I'm going to do something; it bothers me if I don't at least try. We also were taught to pay back a debt, regardless of how small it was. If someone lends you even a quarter, pay it back. You will amaze all of your friends and family who loan you money! I promise.

Nino and I took music and dancing lessons, and he started taking clarinet lessons. We appeared in countless recitals and won all sorts of talent contests until there was nothing more for us to prove in Niagara Falls. Whenever Mom learned about a contest, we signed up and usually won it. That also happened in Buffalo since we were only fourteen miles away. An easy ride.

I remember some talk about moving to LA, where we could really have a chance at success, but it was just mild talk. However, we did take a trip to New York City. Mom lined up some top agents and managers. After watching us perform and seeing write-ups, they all said the same thing: Nino and I were extremely talented, and I had a rare and identifiable and lovely voice, but if we stayed in Niagara Falls, nothing substantial would ever come from it. That was for certain.

One important agent said, "You realize Carol is of an age where she will be propositioned, and they will tell her if she goes the sex route and gives in, things can happen faster. You must be aware of that. It happens often."

"I would never let that happen," I said. "Never! I don't believe that happens to everyone—only to the ones who want it. I have talent and wouldn't do it!" Thankfully, no one ever approached me with such a proposition.

When Nino won the popular *Major Bowes Amateur Hour* on the radio, he and Mom went back to New York City, and the agents repeated the same line—we had to leave Niagara Falls if we ever expected to make something of our talent.

Dad had a friend from Niagara Falls, Carmen Maro, who moved to San Jose, California, after he married. He loved it there but came back to visit his family in Niagara Falls for a few months every few years. In this particular year, 1940, Carmen and Dad were talking, and Dad told him that he and Mom had discussed the possibility of moving to Los Angeles because of Nino and me. Well, Carmen was an extremely persuasive man. It wasn't difficult to talk Dad into leaving, for he also believed in our talent. Dad was young, adventuresome, and happy, for he had captured and married the most beautiful girl he had ever seen; he would do whatever Mom wanted.

Mom and Dad talked it over and decided to move to LA. They sold the successful grocery store, gave up the new apartment we had moved into a year earlier, gave the piano away (thank god), packed up, and drove to Los Angeles. Can you believe it? I was overjoyed and too caught up in the moment to realize what a serious move it was.

Mom wanted us to have a chance. She knew we had whatever it took to make it. She was the force behind us! However, the rest of our family did not understand. They wondered how we could even consider leaving them and our home and fly on a dream that, in their eyes, was an impossibility? In spite of constant opposition mixed with love and tears, Mom mustered all of her confidence and said, "They will make it!" Off we went. I look back now and think how very courageous my parents were. How did they do it?

Everyone was in the street the morning we left Niagara Falls. Even Carmen Maro and his wife and his brother were leaving in their car for San Jose, so we had company along the road. What a scene it was! All of our families and friends were there in front of my grandparents' restaurant to say good-bye through loads of tears, good wishes, and hugging and kissing. I couldn't believe we knew so many people. It was like all of Niagara Falls was on the street that morning.

As our adventure began, Nino sat up front with Dad, and Mom and I were in the back. It was a nice car. Dad loved Cadillacs. Right away, Nino assured Dad that if he fell asleep while driving, Nino would nudge him awake. "Don't worry," he said. "I'll be watching you, Dad." In less than forty-five minutes, Mom and I didn't see Nino's head any longer. He was over to the side, asleep. We all laughed, except Nino. He was sleeping.

All along the long drive from New York to California, we stopped many times to eat and to sleep each night in motels (or cabins, as they were called then). Dad was an early riser, so he got up and was ready to go at 5:00 or 6:00 a.m. Mom and I slept in the backseat each morning with our pillows, and Nino, the watcher, sat in the front seat with Dad, sleeping.

Sometimes after breakfast, Mom sat in the front seat with Dad, and Nino and I arm wrestled a bit in the backseat, but most of the time we harmonized many, many songs together. We knew the songs and just began singing.

We loved the way the Mexican mariachis sang their songs, and we tried to imitate them, along with country and western songs. Our voices sounded good to our ears, so we just kept on singing. In 1962, when we started recording and having hits, a disc jockey described our singing as kind of a rock, Italian, country sound. I wonder why.

I saw many cowboys along the way, and they all had blue eyes! I just knew I was headed in the right direction.

As expected, we all loved Los Angeles's warm tropical weather, the greatest weather in the entire world—blue skies and palm trees all year long. I was a great fan of Dorothy Lamour at that time and always wore a flower in my long hair as she did in her movies. I wouldn't even take the garbage out without my flower on, even though Nino made fun of me—but he always made fun of me, and still does, and we still laugh.

CHAPTER 4

California

When we first arrived in LA, we lived with friends from Niagara Falls for a few weeks. They lived in the West Lake Park area. We then found a small, four-room apartment over a garage on Carondelet Street. I went to Virgil Junior High and then to Belmont High School, where I was voted Most Likely to Succeed. I sang "That Old Black Magic" in one of their recitals. I wore a black velvet gown. I must have been about thirteen or fourteen.

During my high school years, I had two very close friends, Joan Baratta and Marlys Flaten. We did everything together. At that early age, every now and then I liked to wear tops that showed a little bit of cleavage. My mom didn't like it, and Joan and Marlys would wait for me at school with a sweater to cover me! Even the boys at school began to ask me why. "You aren't like that." Some of them said that it gave the wrong impression, and I realized that what they were saying was true. I can be stubborn, but I do listen. Mom used to say that she could always talk to me and could often change my mind, but if Nino said no, he meant no, and there was no changing it. How true!

The first years in Los Angeles went by very quickly. We were all homesick. We made friends, and we were busy, but we missed all of our family at home. Dad especially missed the camaraderie of my aunts and uncles. When we lived back east, he would stop by to see them and have coffee and talk a bit on his day off from work. He missed that.

So during school vacation, we gave up our apartment, Dad quit his job, and we all got in the car and drove back to Niagara Falls. I think back now and realize it wasn't like going around the corner. It was three thousand miles away! I believe that we really didn't know how we would feel seeing everyone again or what the trip home really meant. But let me tell you, it was the warmest feeling to see all of the love and joy in the faces that greeted us. We stayed in one of Nonno's empty apartments, and before I knew it, I was going to Niagara Fall High School, and Nino was going to junior high. And we didn't know if this was a vacation or what?, "What happened?"

Then as days passed, we all got the feeling that we really belonged back in California if we wanted to accomplish anything with our careers. Even Dad felt that Niagara Falls was not the same after living in Los Angeles.

. We were back in Los Angeles and decided we would stay with it. We moved into a small, rented house in a courtyard with about nine other houses on a street named, of all things, Normal Avenue. That was a wild misnomer.

Mom kept us busy. Nino had small parts in movies, and he studied the clarinet and saxophone with an exceptional and well-known teacher from a symphony orchestra. The man was so excited about Nino's talent that he decided he would be his only student.

I made some demonstration records for aspiring songwriters and enjoyed it. The songs, of course, were new to me. I memorized the melodies—my good ear came in handy.

I always loved pretty clothes, lovely lingerie, and gardenia cologne. In the early years, I couldn't afford the lovely creations I saw in *Vogue* magazine. One of Mom's sisters, Isabel DeRosa, was a wonderful seamstress and designer. For a few years, we would fly her out to California, and she would sew many great gowns and dresses and blouses for me. We would pick them out of the magazine or design them. We would then buy the fabric, and before I knew it, she had the clothes finished. We couldn't continue this routine for too many years because I was getting busier, and she had a family in Niagara Falls that needed her there. She just had a magic touch, and I wish I could have kept her forever. Mom could also sew and made me some lovely little dresses, but soon I had to hire a regular seamstress.

The super star Mickey Rooney came to the house once regarding some songs he had written. He was quite a talker. It was dinnertime, but he just kept talking! Dad came home and was speechless to find Mickey Rooney in our living room.

In about 1948, I entered a singing contest called the Make-Believe Ballroom Girl put on by Al Jarvis, a prominent disc jockey at KLAC radio in Los Angeles. I won, along with a wonderful black singer whose name was Mary Lou Williams. We split the prize money equally. The judges were the great Lucille Ball, Desi Arnaz, and Charles Bickford. The biggest thrill for us was meeting them.

In 1950, at the young age of fifty-nine, my sweet nonna passed away. Her illness eluded the doctors; they weren't sure if she had leukemia or an infected spleen. In any event, Mom rushed to Niagara Falls. It was a sad time for all of us. She was so sweet and giving and only visited us once while we were in California. She loved it and compared it with Sicily, with the temperate weather and all the fruit trees.

Nino and I were entertaining once a week at the Veterans Hospital in Beverly Hills, close to Santa Monica. I was about seventeen, and Nino was eleven. When we arrived there for the first time, we were introduced to the most handsome man I had ever seen. His name was Leigh Sterling, and he was the master of ceremonies. He was forty-four years old, stood six feet two, and had salt and pepper hair and very prominent blue eyes. He had on a gray suit and black tie and looked sort of like Walter Pidgeon—a very, very handsome movie star. I kept looking at him and told Mom, "He is so beautiful. He's looking over here! He's looking at you, Mom." She said, "No, he's looking at you!" I couldn't and wouldn't believe it. Everyone stared at Mom because she was so pretty. Even I stared at her. It wasn't until he called us on the phone and came over to our little house in the courtyard for dinner quite a few times that I realized he might be coming to see me. I did know that he loved Mom's cooking, especially when she made fried potatoes and peppers and onions.

On Monday nights, Nino and I took the bus and met Leigh on Canon Drive in Beverly Hills, where he picked us up and took us to do the show at the Veterans Hospital. He then drove us home.

Leigh loved emceeing the show. He was a great showman. He got a kick out of singing like Al Jolson, imitating people, and clowning around. He introduced me on the first night, and from then on, as the "pièce de résistance." He loved my singing and thought Nino was very talented.

One night during the show, Nino was onstage, and Leigh and I were watching him from backstage. Nino was tap-dancing when I noticed he had on one yellow sock and one red sock. How we laughed! One night, Leigh asked Mom and Dad if he could take me to the Club Gala on Sunset Strip to hear Bobby Short sing and play the piano. Bobby was very popular at that time, and I wanted to see him perform. He executed songs with his particular phrasing. I had a wonderful time. We went there twice while he was in town, and I learned quite a lot about his singing technique and became a fan of his. I learned to pay attention to the words and that the story was so important!

Leigh was in the vitamin business, and he spent much of his time in Europe. He always wrote to us while he was away. My family was very close to him, especially Nino. We trusted him implicitly. He picked me up once when I had to sing in Covina and needed a ride home, and when he dropped me off at the house, he kissed me in the car. This was the second time he had kissed me in the car. The first was the last time we went to the Club Gala. I knew what he wanted and hoped for, but that wasn't in my head, and at that point, I had done very little kissing and had never even had a steady boyfriend. Leigh had always been a perfect gentleman with me, and I had a big crush on him, but I wasn't anywhere near ready for sex. After kissing me that second night, he said, "I'm just shaking the apple tree a bit. One day, someone will come along and pick the apples."

Strangely, that was the last time I saw him. The next day, I was scheduled to go to the hospital to have a cyst removed from my breast; thankfully, it was benign. Leigh was rushed to the same hospital for indigestion. I asked the nurse about him because I heard he was just down the hall from me, and she said, "He just expired." I realized that "expired" meant that he had died! How could that be? I was inconsolable; I couldn't stop crying. My parents and Nino rushed to the hospital. We couldn't believe that he was gone so fast.

Something he said has helped me through the years. "Be who you are, Carol. Don't change, and you can charm everyone and have anyone and anything you want." I took his advice, and it stayed with me—along with his memory. I still think of him today.

At seventeen, I thought perhaps I should take some singing lessons, but I quit soon after. I didn't like the way the teachers wanted me to hold my mouth open, and I was afraid that they might change my style. Even at a young age, I knew I had something different, and to me that was most important. However, thinking back, I do wish I hadn't been so impatient. I could have made it work by incorporating their suggestions with my style. My style was an untrained voice, rather breathy and husky, especially if I sang softly. I learned to pay great attention to the words of a song. I loved words. I wanted to make my audience feel *something*, whether I sang onstage or on a record. I wanted to pick them up and take them there—wherever the song went.

Mom, Nino, and I got around Los Angeles by bus since Dad was the only driver in the family. He worked for many years at an Italian delicatessen after trying his luck at starting his own Italian grocery store. His attempt failed. It was the wrong location, so he worked for others until his retirement. It wasn't easy, but he never complained.

I was in the eleventh grade in Belmont High School when I got an offer to sing with Hoagy Carmichael's Teenagers orchestra for an engagement at the Russian River Resort in Northern California. Hoagy was the composer of many hit songs, including "Stardust." I accepted, and they furnished a chaperone for me. I don't remember who got me the job. It must have been word of mouth or Mom! The boys in the band were eighteen and nineteen years old. Stan Getz, the great saxophonist, was one of the young men.

We traveled by bus, and one night when they thought I was asleep, I heard the boys talking about the young girls they made out with each night. They made the girls believe they were truly interested in them so they could get what they wanted. I will never forget how they laughed! It upset me. I was seventeen years old and so naive. They teased me unmercifully, but I made them laugh, and they also protected me and were my friends.

One night, I did a show and was sitting on the bandstand, and Dinah Shore was in the audience. They asked her to come up onstage and say a few words. I was so excited to see her and was smiling at her when she came up. She walked right past me and didn't smile or even look at me. It was as though I wasn't there. I was disappointed and thought that if I were ever in her position, I would never snub or ignore another up-and-coming singer—or anyone, for that matter.

CHAPTER 5

April Stevens

I was back in LA looking for some sheet music in the largest music store in Los Angeles, Music City on Sunset and Vine, when two good-looking young, Italian, brown-eyed men approached me and said, "You look like a singer." (How about that for a line?) "Would you be interested in putting your voice on a recording we just cut for our new record company?" They were Tony Sepe and Joe Lanza. I thought for certain they were just flirting, but just in case they were not, I gave them my phone number. I was right on both counts: they did need a voice, and they were flirting! The name of the song was "No, No, No, Not That." I just learned that it was written by Hal David. I'm sure Tony Sepe told me that at the time, but I don't think I would have recognized the name then.

Some of the song's lyrics were, "The moon is much too bright; you're holding me tight. No, no, no, not that." I studied and learned the song at home. The unknown record company was called Laurel Records.

The day we cut the record, Tony Sepe handed me the song, turned off all of the lights in the studio, and told me to sing into the microphone. He said, "Pretend you are in a car parked, and you are with your boyfriend, and he is trying to kiss you."

I didn't have a boyfriend, but I found out that with my natural shyness and voice, I could imagine and act it out very well. When they played back the tape, it surprised even me. I believe that this record and this event with Tony Sepe initiated my style of talking and singing on records. I was very believable.

A few nights later, I was at the Palladium in Hollywood doing a benefit show when Les Brown, the orchestra leader for Bob Hope, came up to me and said, "Carol, Tony played the recording you made for him, and it's very good, but I'm afraid it may be banned because it's very suggestive. Perhaps you should change your name just for this one record." I was using the name Carol Tempo (short for LoTempio), and for just this one record, I thought it was all right to come up with a new name to protect my own.

That night, my aunt Elaine Mancini, my mom's youngest sister, suggested the name April. We both loved the name, and we were both following a comic strip with a girl in the story named April Kent. I was born in April, so maybe it would be lucky for this one record. Stevens was just a thought, and it sort of went with April, but I hadn't really decided on a last name. April Kent didn't sound like a singer.

We couldn't decide on a last name, Sterling or Stevens. We decided it would wait until the next day, but it didn't. Later that night, Tony called and said that they had already pressed the record, and I was now April Stevens! It was a strange feeling, but I shrugged and thought little of it since it was for just one record…or so I thought.

Since there was no distribution or money behind it, "No, No, No, Not That" did not soar to the skies. It did get banned, and I learned quickly that being banned means publicity and notoriety. My name was being talked about—April Stevens!

I was introduced to Al Piantidosi at the Brown Derby in Hollywood. He was a charming man in his seventies and was the composer of many hit songs during the Tin Pan Alley era. He thought that I was the best singer ever and truly believed in my talent almost as much as Mom did.

Nino and I wrote a song with Al Piantidosi called "Don't Do It." A funny scene happened. Al asked me if Nino and I would do a song for a corporate outing that he was affiliated with. I was about nineteen years old, and Nino was about fourteen. Of course, we were not singing together professionally at that early date. The only song we could think of to do was "Don't Do It," the song we wrote with Al, and then Nino could accompany me on the clarinet. At the time, he was taking lessons on the saxophone and clarinet.

Picture this. It was 10:30 in the morning, and the audience was all men. We walked onstage to the podium. It wasn't exactly a stage, but it was a speaking area with a microphone. I walked to the microphone, but it was too tall for me, even though I was standing on a small step. Nino was to the right of me. There wasn't any introduction—complete silence—and then Nino played one note on the clarinet to give me my key. *Toot.* Then I began to sing, "Don't do it, please don't do it. Stop holding my hand." Then Nino played four lonely notes between the stanzas. Then I began to sing, "Don't do it, please don't do it. You don't understand." Nino played the lonely notes again. One note at a time. I was looking at his face and his eyes and started to laugh, and then all hell broke loose. We couldn't contain ourselves any longer. What we were doing up there was so comical and silly. We just doubled over and howled! I mean, we were laughing hysterically with tears. The poor audience just looked up at us as if to say, "What is going on?" Perhaps they did not see the irony of me singing a sexy song to a group of older men at 10:30 in the morning with no band, just a teenager playing a clarinet one note at a time. But we did, and we were hysterical.

We went offstage still laughing. We couldn't stop. I don't think Al Piantidosi ever really forgave us, and I don't blame him.

But Nino and I made sure that *that* never happened again! After our mishap, I don't know why, but I did sign with Al's recording company, Society Records, and cut six or seven songs, including "Don't Do It," "The Sweetest Day," "Night in a Toy Shop," and "Shadow Waltz." Like Laurel Records, the company had very little money behind it, but through it, I did get a call from RCA Victor. (See how it works?) They heard one of my "society records" and wanted to sign me! It was my dream coming true, and I couldn't wait to tell Al. Much to my surprise, he was not happy. I said, "Al, isn't it wonderful? I can't believe they want to sign me, and I definitely want you to manage me and help guide my career. I need you."

And I did. But he would have none of it. He said firmly, "If you leave Society Records, April, we are through." I knew he meant it, but I could not turn down RCA Victor Records. It broke my heart to walk away from him. My final record for Society Records was "A Little Later Perhaps—Not Now."

I was very proud of my Italian heritage. I never would have thought about changing my name. Carol was fine with me. However, in the forties and fifties, ethnic last names were not popular, so we decided to change LoTempio to Tempo. Then I became April Stevens, and I've been April Stevens ever since. I don't believe the new name made it all happen, but I do know it enhanced everything. April was magical for me. That I know. From the beginning, I loved the name April, and now I feel more April than Carol. It inspired me so. Bless my aunt Elaine for thinking of it. It gave me an extra spark and confidence and seemed to lift me up so that I had to live up to the name. All of my immediate family in Niagara Falls still calls me Carol, but otherwise, I'm April.

I couldn't believe I was with RCA Victor and all of the stars who were on the label. My parents were overjoyed about RCA, too. They had worked so hard and made so many changes in their lives for us. I had hits with RCA immediately. The first song, "I'm in Love Again" written by Cole Porter years before, was always recorded in a fast tempo, but Henri Rene, the producer, wanted to arrange it in a slow, languorous style with loads of violins. Henri Rene's name was very large on the record, and mine was way at the bottom. It said "featuring April Stevens" in very small letters.

Because my mom coached me from the booth to *really* feel it, the song came off beautifully. All I really said in the song was "I'm in love again," but I felt like I meant it, and I sang it that way. Oddly, I was not in love and never had been! *Thanks to you, Mom. You pushed me in the right direction, and you were wonderful.* I was on such a high. I was with RCA Victor, and my first record was a hit! What a jolt it was. I get chills just writing about it.

My second song with RCA was the oldie "Gimme a Little Kiss, Will Ya, Huh?" It was a very old song. In fact, I believe it was originally recorded by Betty Boop of "Boop-Oop-a-Doop" fame. My record was banned everywhere except in Houston, Texas.and I don't know why just Houston. In March 1952, I recorded for RCA "I Love the Way You're Breaking My Heart," which was also recorded by Peggy Lee, and "Meant to Tell You," which the popular Johnny Mercer had a hand in writing. Then there was a beautiful song called "And So to Sleep Again." Patti Page originally recorded it, and I followed, so we all competed for airplay. I was in great company.

The mail poured in! My aunt Elaine helped me with it all. She and her husband, Dom, moved to California. There were boxes and boxes of letters—especially from the boys in the Korean War. They were wonderful, heartfelt letters, and many had us crying. It was such a wonderful feeling to read what they had to say and how they reacted to my voice. Here are a few of the phrases they used:

"Your voice sounds as though you have a throat full of angora sweaters, and we love it". Another soldier wrote," *Other girl vocalists sing, but you actually talk to a guy, and boy, the things you say"*! One was from a disc jockey program called *The Voice of the Desert in Saudi Arabia*. "*You are one of our favorite recording artists, and as for the rest of the base, more of your records are requested than any other artist. Please keep them coming. You are doing the morale of this isolated base wonders!* " I can't find the words to explain what it meant to get these letters. Elaine and I answered every one happily.

Soon we gave up our little house on Normal Avenue for a much nicer apartment off of Wilshire Boulevard near the Miracle Mile District. We were there for about six months, and then my grandfather came out to visit us. He loved Los Angeles and said it reminded him a lot of Sicily, so he bought a house on Ingraham Street off Wilshire near La Brea. Then he decided he didn't need a big house, so he sold it to my dad. We told him whenever he came out, he could stay with us, and he did just that.

We loved the house on Ingraham. It was large and beautifully built, and many of our successes happened there. Shortly after we moved there, I took a few lessons from Jack Stern, who, at that time, was one of the most prominent singing coaches. He was an awfully nice man who gave me singing lessons but didn't change my style. He just played the piano, and I sang, and he corrected me in whatever area I needed, such as holding notes longer and emphasizing certain words.

His son, Arthur Hamilton, was a songwriter. One day, he called me and said he had just written a new song that he felt would be great for me. He came over to the house, played it on our piano, and sang it. Somehow, it really didn't hit me, so he gave it to Julie London. The song was "Cry Me a River." It was a big hit, and since that time, years ago, I think every singer in show business except me has sung that song and put it on an album. Turning that song down was a big mistake. I don't remember what I didn't like about it. Maybe I felt it was too sad. Whatever it was, I'm so sorry I didn't record it.

We had a large home and everything was going well. I couldn't believe it! I was on the Billboard charts with Rosemary Clooney, Patti Page, Tony Bennett, and Frank Sinatra. What a great feeling it was! RCA was going after songs with sexy lyrics; they were so wrong. "I'm in Love Again" did not have sexy lyrics; quite the contrary. All I said was "I'm in love again" many, many times, but it was the *way* I said it. I told them to look for good material and love songs and to let my voice and my delivery be the sex element, not the words. I'm sure if I had stayed in the business, we would have eventually found the right songs. I am certain we would have cleared up so many mistakes that we made.

I hired Ray Gilbert to put my act together. He was a very talented songwriter and a funny man. "Zip-a-Dee-Doo-Dah" and "Bahia" were two of his hit songs. He received the Oscar for Best Song for "Zip-a-Dee-Doo-Dah" for the movie *Song of the South*. He was putting acts together for singers, and I needed some help because I was getting offers and interest from many nightclubs around the country. Can you believe that Henry Mancini was the rehearsal pianist at that time? He was such a nice man, very sweet and accommodating. He certainly progressed from that job after he wrote "Moon River" and many other hit songs. What a talented man.

My first job was the El Rancho Hotel in Las Vegas. Victor Borge, the comedic pianist and actor, and I shared the bill. Mom and Dad came along, and it was mind-boggling. I did very well with attendance wherever I appeared, but somehow I didn't feel it was the right choreography for me. It was just too cutesy. I opened with a song called "Oh Gee, Oh Gosh, Oh Golly, I'm in Love" and then "I'm Old Fashioned" and "Autumn Leaves."

I never told anyone, but I had visions of my name being announced from backstage. The lights would go down, and from backstage, I would begin singing something like, "In the shadows, let me come and sing to you," as I walked onstage with the microphone in my hand. That, I thought, was more in keeping with my style. Of course, I never said anything to Ray Gilbert; I wish I would have!

I never really felt fulfilled with any of my acts on a stage early on. They were too light and frivolous. I was capable of so much more. I could really sing and feel, and I wanted to, but I got caught up in the sexual image. Had I stayed in the business, I am sure I would have adjusted to where I should have been. I *know* I would have.

My managers, Gabbe, Lutz and Heller, were very successful at the time. They also booked Liberace and Frankie Laine, and they wanted me. Liberace thought I should open my act lying on a chaise lounge! That didn't sound right either. However, I think it might have been better than what I was doing. He and his mother came to dinner at our house with our manager Seymour Heller and his wife. Libererace (Lee as we called him) was always with his mother at affairs. He was a very charming man and always smiling. He wasn't as flamboyant then as it was early in his career. He wore a plain suit but I did notice he rings were were quite extreme in size. My favorite singer was Nat King Cole. I loved his style and voice, and I carried a small portable record player and his records with me when I traveled so I could play them in my dressing rooms. He created such a wonderful mood for me. He sang the words to a song like he was singing directly to me. I wanted to be a female Nat King Cole. His were the only records I ever bought. He was the best! Once, I saw him driving by in a convertible on Wilshire Blvd. and was so excited..Ella Fitzgerald was my favorite female singer. She had the sweetest sounding voice and Helen Forrest was also a favorite of mine.

I went on my first tour in 1951. My mother went with me, and later, my aunt Elaine joined me. I worked in Denver at the Broadmoor Hotel with Allan Sherman. I shared the bill with George Gobel at the Chase Hotel in St. Louis, Mo. and then at the Oriental Theater in Chicago with Guy Mitchell. Mom was with me. I visited many service camps. I also went to Hawaii with Tennessee Ernie Ford and a group of entertainers. We entertained the boys at Pearl Harbor, and what an overwhelming and grateful audience they were. It was a lot of fun, and Ernie was a very charming, talented man. It was the only trip on which I didn't have a chaperone because there were so many of us in the troupe. When the tour was over, my dad was at the Los Angeles airport to meet me. Tennessee Ernie went up to him and said, "You have a fine girl; you can be proud of her, Mr. Tempo." Dad was happy, and so was I. Ernie said something to me once that implied he would like to get closer, but I completely overlooked it, and he knew I wasn't going there. During that time, I also appeared on *The Ed Sullivan Show* and then *The Perry Como Show*. I couldn't believe this was happening to me. I was so excited—I had been watching these shows for years! My dreams were all coming true! Next, I sang at the Capital Theatre in Washington, DC, sharing the bill with the comedian Joey Foreman. Eddie Fisher was Joey's best friend. He was in the service at the time and stationed in town. He came by often. He had a crush on my aunt Elaine, who was traveling with me at that time. She was so embarrassed, but Eddie was always a gentleman. We would laugh at the way he would look at her.

While we were in Washington, I was asked to take some photos for the newspaper on the steps of the US Capitol building. My aunt and I were very emotional and excited to be sitting on the steps, waiting for the photographers to come. They were about fifteen minutes late, and then I saw two very large black limos drive up filled with photographers.

I said to Elaine, "Wow, somebody really important must be in town." But when the photographers walked toward us, I quietly added, "It must be a slow day in Washington!"

My aunt Elaine was my mom's youngest sister, and we resembled each other quite a bit, so sometimes fans would mistake her for me. That was a compliment for me. She was a doll!

I have always been amazed that the following happened to my aunt Elaine and her husband, Dom. They were tremendous fans of Frank Sinatra. You never walked into their home in the San Fernando Valley that you didn't hear Frank Sinatra singing on a record. Well, in the 1970s, they lived right next door to a dressmaker that sewed clothes for Frank's first wife, Nancy. Would you believe it? Naturally Elaine and Nancy became good friends, and although Nancy is now in her nineties, they still speak on the phone. What a small world it is.

I was—and am—a great fan of Frank Sinatra's. When I was about ten years old in Niagara Falls, the family and I went to see him perform at the Shea Theatre in Buffalo, where he was singing with Tommy Dorsey's orchestra. After the show, we were standing with all of his fans at the stage door when Frank and some men came out.

Mom said, "Carol, ask him for his autograph!" I said no. I was too shy to do that, so she pushed me. There I was, in front of him with a paper and pencil. He smiled at me, signed the paper, and winked. I was so taken aback. He had the bluest eyes I had ever seen. That was the one and only autograph I ever asked for, and if my mom wouldn't have been there, it wouldn't have happened.

Years later in Los Angeles, after my recording success, I was in his company about four times. The first was at a show we were both appearing in. Right away, he called me Stevie. He liked to give people nicknames. The second time, a friend took me to see him record at a studio. Nino was playing sax in the orchestra, and Don Costa was the bandleader. Frank was in a bad mood and was very unkind and abusive to the young electrician that was hooking up all of the wires in the studio. I asked my friend if he would take me home. I just couldn't stand to see that young man's humiliation in front of all of those people; there was no excuse for that. It spoiled my adoration of his talent for many years.

The third time we met was at the Hollywood Palladium. He was with Ava Gardner, and he never looked happier. He called me Stevie and introduced us, she was exquisite. The fourth time Frank was appearing at Caesars Palace in Las Vegas, and Nino was playing sax in a small, handpicked orchestra Frank had appearing with him, along with Don Costa's large orchestra. In the middle of his act, a small stage was electronically rolled out. On it sat the eight handpicked musicians, including Nino. When Frank made the introduction, he said that Nino was a star in his own right and mentioned my name and "Deep Purple." Then he said, "Nino Tempo is my favorite saxophonist." That was something, coming from Frank Sinatra.

Just before the show went on, Nino and I were backstage when Frank was about to go on. Quickly, I said hello and kissed him on the cheek, and then I went out to the audience. I sat up front, directly behind his daughters, Nancy and Tina. The minute Frank came out and started singing, I could see a very shiny spot on his cheek where I had just kissed him. It was my lip-gloss. What a shine! I was mortified.

I listen to him sing today and think, *what a magnificent voice.* So in tune, so rich, with so much feeling. No one can ever compare. I've got all of my adoration back.

I learned at an early age that a military audience was the greatest and the most appreciative. I had my first experience with such an audience in Los Angeles in 1945. I appeared at the famous Hollywood Canteen. I hadn't even started my career and appeared as Carol Lo Tempio. The response I received from the audience was the loudest and most receptive I had ever experienced.

I met Julie London backstage and will never forget her beautiful face. She had the largest eyes I have ever seen. Light hazel, of course!

In 1948, Nino and I entertained every Monday night at the Sawtelle Veterans Home in West Los Angeles. We entertained the veterans there for a few months.

As April Stevens, I entertained our brave marines at Camp Pendleton in Oceanside, California. At that time, I had a hit record titled "I'm in Love Again." They loved it!

I was then asked to sing at Craig Air Force Base in Selma, Alabama, in January 1953. We visited the wounded at the hospital. I was so surprised that they were so happy to see me! I was heartbroken to see them in their condition. It was a tough day to go through. We entertained them, and they loved it all. They were so sweet.

I did other armed forces radio shows in June 1953 and in January 1955; I did live shows at the military bases in and around Pearl Harbor on the island of Oahu, Hawaii.

Nothing was ever as fulfilling for me as entertaining our boys in the armed forces.

CHAPTER 6

Glenn McCarthy

"To know music is to know God twice." I read that phrase many years ago, and it comes to mind often. Yes, I knew music, and I knew how lucky I was, but I still didn't realize—*really* realize—that my gift, my voice, was God-given and that it should be nurtured and polished. I never made the connection; thus, I took it all for granted.

I was a twenty-year-old newcomer in Los Angeles, making my very first record with a major recording company, RCA Victor. "I'm in Love Again" was climbing up the Billboard charts, along with Tony Bennett's "Because of You," Rosemary Clooney's "Come On-a My House," and Mario Lanza's "Be My Love." I can't tell you how glorious it felt to be with RCA Victor Records and to see my records climbing up alongside of all the stars I had been listening to for years. It was a high like no other, especially to see my parents so very happy and so proud.

It was unbelievable! I was truly on my way, *but*…and it was a big *but*…

I was booked at the Shamrock Hotel in Houston, Texas, on April 1, 1952. It was April Fools' Day, and it really was a joke on me. I often wonder what would have happened if I hadn't been booked into the Shamrock Hotel and met Glenn McCarthy.

Mom and I arrived in a cab, and as we approached the hotel, it looked tremendous! When we stood in front of it, it appeared even larger with its long, green awning from the front door onto the street. It must have been more than twenty floors high. It was a very special time in Texas history when it opened on March 17, 1949.

We walked into the new, beautiful lobby, and there by the elevators was a huge painting of the hotel owner, Glenn McCarthy. It was very impressive, and my heart skipped a beat, for he reminded me of John Wayne.

There was no bigger movie star than John Wayne, the Cowboy. I had a crush on him for years. His walk, his talk, his boldness, his roughness—even his drinking was attractive to me. But what most attracted me was his soft side and shyness. That really did me in. And, oh, those blue eyes! Later on, a friend of mine who also knew Glenn McCarthy very well said he worked as an extra on a couple of movies with John Wayne and that the resemblance between the two men was amazing! He said he watched John Wayne play cards on the set with the crew as he often did, and his and Glenn's mannerisms and voice were identical. His hands were extra large and moved and looked exactly like Glenn's.

I now know that on that first day in the hotel lobby, I should have turned around, grabbed our suitcases and Mom, and run for my life, but I didn't. The lobby was so luxurious and compelling, and everyone was very helpful to us and wanted to please us. It was like a fairyland, a dream come true. Practically everything was green in keeping with the shamrock theme: green carpets, pale green drapes, even green and white flowers everywhere.

The entertainment room was called the Emerald Room, and the smaller bar and restaurant was called the Cork Club. Glenn McCarthy was a real Irishman!

The hotel was only three years old in 1952. It was still the talk of the country. Its opening in 1949 was a huge, star-studded affair. Pat O'Brien, Dorothy Lamour (my favorite), and John Carroll were only a few of the movie stars there. The opening was also attended by the elite of Texas. After all, he was Glenn McCarthy, and he seemed to move mountains to reach his goal of making money—lots of it.

He was a wildcatter who came from nothing. A movie was being made about his life, books were being written about him, and the money was rolling in. No matter what he did, he was in the Texas newspapers, the *Houston Chronicle* and the *Houston Press*. Whether it was good news or bad news, he always made the papers!

Glenn Herbert McCarthy was a very powerful, controversial man, and his name was magical at that time, especially in Houston. When I met him, he was forty-four years old. He was born on Christmas Day in 1907 in Beaumont, Texas, two miles from the Spindle Top oil fields. Although he made his money as a wildcatter, years earlier he had worked at a gas station. He married Faustine Lee, and they had four girls and one boy. Faustine was from a very prominent, wealthy family in Houston. Although they married long before he made any real money, Glenn would not take a cent from her family. Faustine's brother, Howard Lee, married Gene Tierney, the movie actress. They divorced, and he then married Hedy Lamarr, another very popular movie star known for her exquisite beauty.

I couldn't believe I was actually appearing in the Emerald Room at the Shamrock Hotel. My salary was higher than I ever received anywhere—thirteen hundred fifty dollars a week for two weeks!

The night I did my first show, I was very nervous, especially when I heard that Glenn McCarthy was in the audience, as he usually attended all openings. With all the normal stress factors, that was an added concern. The show went very well since "I'm in Love Again" and especially "Gimme a Little Kiss, Will Ya,

Huh?" were big hits in Houston, the latter actually having been played on the radio. It was banned in most cities!

Two days before my day off, the phone rang in my suite. It was Glenn McCarthy. He said, "Miss Stevens, I saw your show and enjoyed it very much. I have been asked to judge a beauty contest in Huntsville on Monday, and I thought perhaps you would like to accompany and appear there with me. It's about a fifty-mile trip by car." His voice was very deep and very authoritative, and he spoke very slowly with a slight Texas accent. I accepted, of course, and I was very excited and surprised that he had even called. But then he did say that most acts, when appearing at the Shamrock, made appearances with him.

I knew exactly what I would wear. I had a lilac tweed suit made for me with a lilac velvet collar and cuffs. I wore lilac shoes and carried a lilac bag. It was appropriate for the month of April because it was the season that bluebonnets bloomed in Texas, so the Emerald room had them in large vases on every table. It was a beautiful sight, and lilac or lavender or any shade of purple had always been my favorite color.

I met him the next morning in front of the Shamrock. He walked out of the front door of the hotel with two of his friends behind him as I stood under the dark green awning.

He was a force to behold with his six-foot frame, tough but handsome face, light blue eyes, and curly, sandy-colored hair falling down over his forehead. He had a small mustache and dark sunglasses, and he was dressed impeccably in a suit and tie. It was all a part of his mystique, and it worked!

I put my hand out and said, "So I'm finally going to meet you." As he shook my hand, I saw a slight, confident smile, but there was also shyness behind it, I liked that.

He said nothing! He made certain that I sat in the front seat next to him with one of the other men on my right. The first thing I noticed as he was driving was his legs. With his cowboy boots on, he looked like he was riding a horse! I never have been able to figure that out.

The contest was pleasant, and the girls were beautiful, as they so often are in Texas, though Glenn seemed to find fault with them. He asked, "Why are they mostly all blondes, and why are they so tall and thin?" Perhaps he said that because he was so busy looking at me, and I was just the opposite, I'm sorry to say.

I was very aware of him all evening. He looked at me but was a man of few words, which made him all the more intriguing. He dropped me off in front of the hotel at around 8:30 and said something like, "I'll see you soon." Soon came up fast, and toward the end of my engagement, I had another day off.

Glenn asked me if I would like to see his farm, which was a few miles out. I said yes, and then he asked a friend, Billy Grey, and his girlfriend, Virginia, to come along. Glenn picked me up around 11:00 am, and when his friends got into the car, I could tell they had already been drinking.

We reached the farm around noon, had some lunch, and then around 3:00 p.m., it was drinking time. I didn't touch any liquor and spend most of my time dodging Glenn and then locking myself in the bathroom. I was mad at Glenn and upset that he kept on drinking. Around 11:00 p.m., Virginia knocked on the door to use the bathroom, and she gave me a sort of disgusted look as I went out. Everyone was drunk and asleep—and not a phone anywhere! I knew Mom would be frantic. I was close to tears and went back into the bathroom and looked out the window at the cows. Yes, cows.

Then I realized everyone out there was useless until they slept it off, so I went out to the front room until just before daybreak and shook Glenn awake and told him my mom would be furious—and who knew who she had called. So they all got up quickly, and in a short while, we were in the car on the highway.

There were no other cars on the desolate two-lane road, but I noticed that Glenn was still sort of out of it, and I said, "Glenn, you're driving on the wrong side of the road." He just looked at me with his usual grin. Soon a policeman stopped us, and when he saw who was driving, he just let us go. That incident did not make the newspapers.

Mom, of course, had been up all night and called the police. I knew she would. I told her exactly what had happened, and she was so mad! There was an article in the paper that day in Walter Winchell's column that said, *"Her reputation has always been beyond reproach, but word has it that April Stevens and Glenn McCarthy are a twosome."*

That night after the show, there was a party in the hotel that Mom and I were invited to. After dinner, Glenn showed up in a white suit and stood in the doorway for all eyes to see. He spotted us, walked directly to Mom, and asked her to dance. While they were dancing, he immediately said to her, "You called the police on me?" She said, "Yes, of course I did! You've got a precious girl there, and I will not let you treat her like this!" He agreed and apologized.

In Bryan Burrough's book, *The Big Rich: The Rise and Fall of the Greatest Texas Oil Fortunes,* a geologist named Michel T. Halbouty wrote that Glenn was "a man inclined to raise his fists at every affront whether large, small, or imaginary…But he could charm Lady Godiva off her horse." (And me off the charts?) Glenn was dynamic, and I admit I was no match.

I met him on April 1, 1952, and on April 29, my birthday, he mailed me a copy of Wallace Davis's book, *Corduroy Road,* based on his life.

He sent me a copy with the inscription, *To April Stevens—the most gracious and lovely lady I ever met.* The movie *Giant,* based on the book written by Edna Ferber, used Glenn's life in the part of Jett Rink. He also sent a TV set to my family's home in Los Angeles. It was large and beautiful—our first television.

The next three months were very busy for me. I had many personal appearances scheduled at clubs and hotels all over the country, and Glenn usually flew in for them. He owned a plane, an Aero Commander, and had a pilot, and that was all he needed.

It was not easy to sing onstage with him in the audience. He was drinking, as usual, but not very heavily, and I was very aware of his presence. I heard him raise his voice a few times, but I kept right on singing.

He tried his best to get to me at every opportunity. We would lie on the bed, kiss, and hold one another. He was quite a handful. But having been brought up as I had, in a very strict, Italian Catholic family, I just couldn't let go and let it happen.

He would come to see me at my appearances and would start trouble with the audience when he was drinking and being loud and annoying. He actually fought with a man one time when the man tried to quiet him. Another time, he got up from his table while I was onstage and went into the showgirls' dressing room and tore up all of their stockings and outfits. It was a mess! All because he hated my being in show business! I was so apologetic to the girls and the owner, but of course Glenn paid for the damage—and then some.

In July 1952, I was booked into the Del Mar Hotel in California. He flew in for the show. Mom was with me. I had a feeling I wasn't going to be able to control or pacify him. I didn't have any reason, but I did feel I was in for a confrontation. I told Mom after the show that I was going to see him for a short while and would be right back. I walked to his suite, and I knew my suspicions were right. I could tell by the look on his face that I wasn't going to talk my way out of this. Three months was enough. He looked worn out and determined, and he said, "April, I can't go on this way any longer if we are going to continue."

And I knew I couldn't even imagine my life without him in it, so we made love. With Mom down the hall, and with years of caution hammered into my brain, it was a bittersweet experience. I didn't get to experience a joyous ceremony in which I could tell the world how crazy I was about him and how much in love I was. This wasn't how I had imagined losing my virginity would be, so no wonder it wasn't the ecstasy I had heard so much about. But as time went by, I was in heaven.

From that time on, for almost seven years, the phone calls began every day by 4:00 p.m. He sometimes called at night, too. No matter where I was, I was home by 4:00. There were no cell phones back then, so it was different.

For the almost seven years I saw him, he didn't want me to learn to drive. I suppose he felt it would be too much freedom for me. He made sure to call me without fail at 4:00pm every day; I wrote to him every night, and he wrote at least three or four long letters every week.

During my time with Glenn, I met and became very friendly with two sisters around my age, Joan and Doris Barton and we grew inseparable. Their family name was Castagna, and they were movie extras and had no desire to go any further in the movie business.

We could never figure out who was the prettiest—they were both so lovely. Joan was going with Glenn's brother, Bill McCarthy, at the time, and the four of us were always together—traveling, partying, and laughing hysterically. Joan and Doris's family became very close to mine. We share so many funny stories that even now, we go over them on the phone and laugh.

Once, Glenn was flying in to see me. Since I had such a high forehead and complained of it so often, Joan suggested that I should wear straight bangs to cover it. So I gladly went to her hairdresser to have him put a straightening solution on my bangs because my hair was very wavy. Well, for some reason, the solution didn't work; in fact, it produced reverse results. So I had this fuzz on my forehead when I went to meet Glenn. Very funny—but not for me.

CHAPTER 7

Back to the Shamrock

In January 1953, I again appeared at the Shamrock Hotel for two weeks. This time, they featured a radio show called *Saturday at the Shamrock* with the star appearing at the hotel. Humphrey Bogart was in town after winning the Academy Award for the movie *The African Queen*. He was there to appear on the show with me and to sing "Gimme a Little Kiss, Will Ya, Huh?" with me. I couldn't believe it was happening. He was a very kind, sweet man, which surprised me, I guess, because most of his roles in the movies were so serious.

We each had a script, and the host was a man named Fred Nehas from the hotel. Secretly, I had a good laugh when Fred would correct Humphrey Bogart on how to say a certain line. He went over it several times, and I wanted to say, "Fred! For God's sake, he just won an Academy Award!" But Bogie was a gentleman throughout it all. So I had to be a lady.

After the radio show, he got a phone call, and when he came back, he laughed and said, "It was my wife, Betty [Lauren Bacall]. She just heard the two of us singing together." We both laughed. Later that night, after my performance in the Emerald Room, we sat together to take pictures, and he said, "April, I hear you are seeing Glenn McCarthy. Why would you do that?

You have a great career ahead of you, and you know the stories about him." I just looked at him with a lump in my throat and wanted to cry.

As I said, I appeared at the Shamrock Hotel for the second time in January 1953. This time, instead of doing two shows nightly, Glenn decided I should do only one. He didn't want me to leave the suite to do the other show. I couldn't believe it! And then, I had to argue with him to do even one show! I kept saying, "But this is your hotel—you are the boss! How can you ask me not to do a show?" It was beginning to be impossible. I don't think he was thinking clearly. And I *know* he was drinking more.

I hired a pianist, Paul Marco, to travel with me and to help me rehearse the orchestras since it was too much for me to try to do alone. It was a big help, and the shows were much better; in addition, Mom didn't have to leave Dad to travel with me. Glenn, of course, resented Paul because he was so handsome. He said, "Did you have to pick the best-looking pianist in the world?" Paul was a really nice guy and good pianist who just happened to be very handsome. He had dark hair and eyes and was very Italian looking. Glenn knew there was nothing going on with Paul, but when he was drinking, he wasn't so sure. He was a bad drinker. If he had just a few drinks, as he usually did, he would be charming and playful. But more than that and he was a terror! He conjured up all sorts of things in his mind.

I flew back and forth to Houston whenever I could and stayed three or four days in his suite with him. And every two weeks or sooner, he would fly to wherever I was appearing or to Los Angeles and the Beverly Hills Hotel, where he always stayed. I never stayed with him overnight when he was in Los Angeles. I could not do that. I don't know what Mom and Dad thought, but they were very kind at that time. They knew how much he meant to me, and he came to our house for dinner in Los Angeles many times. He told them he was serious about me but that he couldn't get the divorce. His wife, Faustine, would have to initiate it. It was during the time that wives, not husbands, sought divorces. That was what he told me, anyway. She came very close to doing it at one point. She hired attorneys, and it made the front page of the newspapers, but then a close family member died and she stopped the proceedings and never did pick them up again.

During our time together, he bought me a beautiful emerald-cut diamond ring. He said it was not an engagement ring and not to wear it on my left hand yet. So I wore it on my right hand, and there it stayed.

On my second engagement at the Shamrock, I was with Glenn outside of the hotel when we ran into Faustine and their daughter, Glenna Lee. They were fine to me, but Faustine was very cold to Glenn. It hurt so much to see them that I cried later up in his suite, saying, "What is wrong with you? They are such beautiful and lovely people." He said, "You don't understand" and of course I didn't, but I should have.

Another time when I was visiting Glenn in Houston, his eleven-year-old son, Glenn Jr., came to the door. I went into the bedroom when I heard who it was. He was crying his eyes out, saying, "I know she's here Daddy. I know April's here." When he left, Glenn came into the bedroom to find me in tears and he said, "Now I've got you both crying." Of course, I knew how wrong it all was, but I truly believed that we could be happy together. How foolish I was.

When I quit the business in early 1955, of course my income stopped. He would hand me about three hundred dollars every few weeks. At first I wouldn't take it, but later he insisted. Then I would go shopping and spend it all on shirts and ties and sweaters for him.

I thought about my parents and what they had given up for me, but they seemed happy that I was truly in love. I'm certain, though, that in their heart of hearts, they wished I hadn't given up my dreams—and their dreams—when I was so close. I was actually there.

My manager at the time was Stanley Styne, the son of Jule Styne, the famous songwriter. When he came to our home, I told him I was quitting and why, and he tried to talk me out of it for hours. Finally, he said, "You'll be back!" I can recall that evening as if it were yesterday.

The famous writer, Edna Ferber, wrote *Giant* based on Glenn's life, and it was made into a movie. In 1956, Glenn and I went to see it. The first thing he said pertaining to James Dean was, "Is that *little* guy supposed to be me?" I'm not certain Glenn knew exactly who James Dean was. He may not have known that he was the biggest star in Hollywood at that time. James Dean was a beautiful man. His style and acting ability put him in the same class as legends Marlon Brando and Marilyn Monroe.

I guess Glenn thought that big, tall Rock Hudson was going to portray him. He was so disappointed that he kept grunting all through the movie, so it was difficult for me to enjoy it or give you a true critique of it.

I was on a double date once with Rock Hudson. (I was with the other fellow.) Rock Hudson was then Roy Sherer Jr., a nice, friendly, very handsome guy. A few years later, he called to congratulate me on my first hit record, "I'm in Love Again." He had changed his name to Rock Hudson. I congratulated him, also, on his great success in the movies. I was so happy for him.

Glenn and I would often travel to Las Vegas for a weekend. He loved to gamble, especially shooting dice. He won a lot and lost a lot. We also often flew in his plane to Mexico City, Oklahoma City, Chicago, and Palm Springs. Sometimes he would send his plane to Los Angeles to pick me up. I didn't like to be on the plane alone. It was a strange feeling. He asked me once, "What were you drinking on the plane on the way over?" I said, "Milk." He laughed and thought that was funny. I guess it was funny, considering.

I now think of him and wonder what strong attraction drew me to him enough to give up my dreams. He had magnetism, looks, and power, and he was my first love. I believe what I loved most about him was his playfulness and how we laughed together. But then I remember my mother always said, "When it comes to men, respect has to be at the top of the list." When she first told me this, I wondered what respect had to do with anything. Now I know so well. At the time of my affair, I didn't respect Glenn or myself. I knew we were both doing wrong. His drinking to the extreme began to bother me, and he wasn't going to the office as often as usual.

Once, I was in his suite and got a call from the manager of the famous Cork Club, the Shamrock's bar and restaurant. He said "Miss Stevens, Mr. McCarthy asked if you could please come down here as soon as you can." I said, "Of course, I'll be down in a few minutes." I walked in, and everyone at the bar looked at me, but I didn't see Glenn. The manager then walked me to a large table in the middle of the room and lifted up the tablecloth. There sat Glenn with a drink in his hand, a little smile on his face, and his hair messed up. I couldn't believe that he was literally under the table. He said, "What kept you?" He pulled me under the table with him, and there we both sat and laughed until we ached.

When we stayed in, we ordered room service or cooked in the kitchen. If I cooked spaghetti sauce, he would drop bananas in it to make me mad! He was an awful cook, and I made only spaghetti!

Another time, I was in the suite, expecting him to come in at the usual time to shower and change and take me to dinner. I hid behind a large chair in the bedroom and of course expected him to call me or look for me. He came in, went into the bathroom, showered, dressed, made a phone call, and then walked out to the lobby. I was crushed! I ran out the door into the lobby and said, "Did you actually forget I was here? You didn't even look for me!" He turned around, laughing, and we fell into each other's arms. It seemed he always outplayed me. He always said I amused him. That didn't surprise me, but at what a cost.

I never spent more than four or five days with him, with one exception. We went to his ranch in Uvalde, Texas. My brother, Nino, and my aunt Elaine and her husband, Dom Mancini, went with us for nine or ten days. It was a fun trip; the ranch house was rough and rugged looking but very accommodating. It had four or five bedrooms and baths and a large kitchen. The front room walls were covered with deer and goat heads, and all kinds of skins were on the couches and chairs. We hunted at night in a jeep with spotlights on the animals. I only went out hunting twice. I didn't feel it was a fair game for the animals, and I didn't enjoy it. I began to notice then that he wasn't a fair man.

I had my own bedroom at the ranch, but we got together when everyone else was sleeping. I felt rather embarrassed in the morning, but Nino, Elaine, and Dom at least seemed to be unaware. I believe they were making it easy for me; they knew how much I truly loved him. We all took a turn cooking; that was fun, and the ten days flew by. Glenn made ice cream for us, and it was delicious!

Glenn and I had a lot of arguments. While I was visiting him in Houston, for instance, he would accuse me of flirting with our waiter while ordering dinner. I would naturally get angry because it was absurd. I would pack my clothes, and fly back to Los Angeles. Then he would call me and apologize, and I would fly back to Houston. He used to say I was obstinate and rambunctious. Once, I said he was unfair! He then looked straight into my eyes, and with all of the fire and strength he had in him, he said, "I'm not fair!" I'll never forget that look. It was like he was trying to tell me something! He always seemed to think I was looking at other men, and I never was! That was the furthest thought from my mind. Why would I ever look at another man with him in my life? It was a puzzle for me then.

Although I had been out of show business for a few years, I got an offer from Columbia Pictures saying they had heard a record of mine and wanted to use my singing voice for Rita Hayworth's voice in her movies. I thought it was a great opportunity, as did my family, because there would be no traveling. Just singing in a studio in LA, dubbing my voice, and being well paid for it. But Glenn was upset, naturally. He said Rita Hayworth always played sexy roles and was a woman of ill repute, and he didn't want me associated with that kind of person. That really hurt me, but again I went along.

All the while we were together, from 1952 to 1959, Glenn was going back and forth to Bolivia looking for oil wells, but there were no discoveries. I never did go with him on any of his trips there, but he did bring me back some lovely vicuna material, and I had a suit and coat made.

I believe I felt the decline happening. Glenn was drinking more and going to the office less; things were not going as well as they had been for him. In 1955, three years after Glenn and I met, Nino said, "Carol, leave him. I know it will hurt, but leave him right now! I know what I'm talking about, and if he doesn't come after you with a solid plan and with a date, you will get your answer and save yourself a lot of time." God, how I wish I could have done that, but my feet wouldn't move. I was stuck to him!

Time went on, and we continued, but I was beginning to feel the pain and fear that the possibility of losing brings. I couldn't imagine my life without him, and I really believed he wanted what I did. He said we should have children because that would always hold us together. I wondered about that remark. Sometimes when you wait too long, too much time goes by, and everything disappears. It was then I knew the end was coming.

My grandfather was visiting, and in the past he had met Glenn a few times and had dinner with us at the house. He even invested a small amount of money in Glenn's Bolivian deals. He lost the investment, of course, but they were friendly. On this particular visit, my grandfather said, very straightforward, "Girly, I don't think the cowboy is going to be able to get a divorce." Then Nino hit me with, "This has got to stop!" Of course I knew he was right. It had gone on for too many years.

It all just stopped. No phone calls, no letters in either direction. Everything stopped, except the anguish, which came on with a vengeance! What pain I felt, missing him and knowing, really knowing it was over, plus the guilt and the years gone from my life. My parents and Nino were devastated! No one in the business at that time even answered my calls. Mom screamed at Glenn for what he did until I had to stop her. I said, "Don't blame him alone. It was my fault, too! I allowed it!" I then looked in the hallway mirror, pointed to my face, and said, "You allowed it!" And that was the truth.

Friends of my brothers wanted me to sue Glenn for all of the money I would have made had he not stopped me from working for all those years. I knew there was some validity to what they said, but I couldn't do it. I loved him, and after all, I had allowed it to happen. My dad took it easy on me. I'm certain he didn't want me to feel any worse than I already did. But Mom raged, saying, "You don't deserve to have been given such a great gift. You have no idea how rare it is, and to have tossed it away for a married man, for all these years." It was awful, but she was so right (as she always was).

Between the tears, I finally decided I was not going to feel sorry for myself. I'd wasted enough time. Nino was busy with his saxophone, working with the Lighthouse All-Stars, Maynard Ferguson's band, and recording sessions he was contracted to play in. I had a lot of bad days, but I would try to talk to myself and pick myself up. I had done it to myself, it was over, and I had to go on.

There was one phone call. It was brief and very sad, and I remember Glenn saying, "I've done enough harm to you."

Shortly after my grandfather warned me about Glenn, he went back to Niagara Falls and passed away from a heart attack. We knew he had heart problems, but he always seemed indestructible. It was an unhappy time for all of us, but losing him was the worst. He was seventy-two years old.

I didn't date for over a year. I couldn't do it. I still felt in my heart that I belonged to Glenn. I had never had a boyfriend to that extent, and I could never imagine myself married to anyone. I don't know why. I had a lot of boyfriends and relationships later on, but I was always disappointed. I found it difficult to find all the important elements in one man, and again, Mom was right. Respect was on top of the list.

I never got serious about anyone. Something was always wrong or missing. I was very intent on trying to build my career again.

Joan finally married Bill for about eight years, and then they divorced. During their marriage, they lived part of the time in Houston. We talked often on the phone, and one time, she said she noticed that after about a year, Glenn began to take out one of his secretaries, and Joan remarked to him that the woman reminded her of me. Glenn said, "Yes, I know, but she's only a shadow of April."

During that same time, the girls and I were friendly with La Rue Katzman. It was just before her husband, Lennie Katzman, came up with the idea to write the infamous television show *Dallas*. He was so fond of my name that he called one of the women in the cast of *Dallas* April Stevens.

Joan is now married to George Kennedy, the actor, and lives in Boise, Idaho. Although we do talk on the phone, my time with Joan and Doris long ago was most memorable, and I love them and miss them in my life.

CHAPTER 8

Learning to Drive

I was almost thirty years old after my affair with Glenn, and I had not yet learned to drive. To learn became my first serious objective, so I took driving lessons and then practiced with Dad and Nino. I was never very mechanically inclined, and I think driving a car is a bit in that category, with directions and all. I passed my writing test and assumed I was ready for the driving test. I was wrong.

On that day, I went to the school and got in the car, with an instructor sitting next to me. We were behind the school, and I was about to pull out of the driveway into the street. I was nervous as all hell! Suddenly, out of nowhere, a mailman carrying his bag appeared on the sidewalk just as I was making my way into the street. I barely missed him, and I immediately slammed on the brakes as he yelled, "Learn how to drive, lady!"

That was not good. The instructor was pretty shaken up and said, "I think he's right. You should go home and practice." Later, I did finally get my driver's license, and became a good driver with one exception: I had trouble with my left turns. I could never figure out who had the right of way. In those days, we didn't have signals with green arrows that told you when to go and when to stop. I would drive into the left-hand lane and then go out a bit so the car on the opposite side of the street was facing me. I would then look into the driver's eyes only to be met with a look of extreme confusion.

I decided not to risk left turns, so whenever I had to go someplace, I would map it all out on a piece of paper that required me to make only right-hand turns. It was possible, but it took *forever* to go anyplace! When I went on my little trips, my dad would watch for my return from the house. When he saw me drive up, he'd yell to Mom, "Hon, she made it." I've been driving now for years and absolutely love it, but I am still a little leery of left turns.

You know, of all the years I was with Mom and Dad, and there were many, I never, ever heard them call each other by their first names, Ann and Sam. It was always "hon" or honey. They would refer to other people by their given names, but they never addressed each other or spoke or wrote a letter or note by any name but hon.

CHAPTER 9

Cary Grant

I finally began to get a few people in the business to answer my phone calls, and I learned that I was on a list of *Billboard* magazine's important popular singers. Of all the top female vocalists, I was chosen as the one with the biggest drop in my career in the last few years. Frank Sinatra was number one on the male list at a time; his career was at an all-time low. At least I was in good company, but we were both at the bottom!

In 1958, Nino got a small part in the movie *Operation Petticoat* with Cary Grant and Tony Curtis. It was shot in Florida and took a few months to make. When they all returned to Los Angeles, Nino and a few of his friends from the film, including Cary Grant, went horseback riding. The plan was, as Nino told Mom and Dad, that three of them would come back with Nino to our home to have a spaghetti dinner with us. Nino and I both often invited friends for dinner at the last minute—poor Mom and Dad. Actually, I think they enjoyed it because we brought home colorful people from show business that were lots of fun, and they did love the wonderful food Mom cooked.

On this particular day, Nino was giving directions to the house, and Cary just stood off in the distance, listening. So, Nino said, not thinking that Cary would accept, "Cary, you wouldn't like to come for dinner too, would you?" Cary got a big smile on his face and said, "Why, of course, Nino. I would love to." Nino was astounded and said, "Great! OK, just follow me in the car, but first I've got to make a phone call."

What a phone call that was! He called and told us what happened and that Cary Grant was coming to dinner, too. Mom dropped the wooden spoon she was stirring with at the stove, Dad's mouth popped open and stayed that way, and I started to laugh. It was all too funny. But then Nino said the funniest thing of all. "Please, please, try to act natural! Don't get excited, and don't act like he's a star or stare at him."

That was impossible! He was a star—and the biggest! We had never met a star of his caliber, and he was the nicest, kindest man we had ever met. We all fell in love with him.

When he walked in, I was still giggling out of nervousness, I guess. His arms were full of crème de cacao brandy bottles, and our Doberman pinscher, Zach, somehow got out of the guest bedroom when someone opened the door to put his or her jacket on the bed, and he came dashing in as Cary was bending over, putting the bottles on the table. Zach goosed him with his nose, and Cary said, "Hey, you, cut that out!" Exact words!

We all roared with laughter, Nino put Zach away, and with that we began a wonderful relationship with Cary Grant. For years, until he passed away, he would come at least three or four times a year for spaghetti dinner. At first, he would bring a date, and then he brought his wife, Dyan Cannon, and their baby girl, Jennifer, and then his new wife, Barbara. He always called on the holidays or on our birthdays. He and Dyan took Nino and me to a baseball game once. Some fans rushed up to us and asked for our autographs. We were embarrassed that they didn't recognize Cary, but he just laughed. What a guy. He was the best.

Nino and I were working at Harrah's in Reno on my birthday. The phone rang. When I answered, a voice said, "Hello, April. This is Cary Grant, and I just spoke to your mom, and I want to wish you a happy birthday." For years, Nino had been imitating Cary's voice, saying "Judy, Judy, Judy," so I thought the phone call was from Nino, teasing me because Cary never called us on the road before. When I realized it was really Cary Grant, I couldn't thank him enough and told him, "You made my day." And he had. What a sweet, thoughtful man. Ironically, he never had a leading lady named Judy.

Cary invited the four of us to his house for dinner. Eva Marie Saint and her and husband were there. They were very congenial. He had just finished the movie *North by Northwest* with her. I had just seen the movie, so it was so strange to be sitting across from them.

When we won the Grammy Award, Cary came to the cocktail party that Atlantic Records gave for us and sat at our table all night. He was such a good friend, and we truly miss him in our lives. He told Nino some little gems I'd like to pass on so you will know what a considerate, fine man he was. He once said, "People don't always think to invite me on special occasions because they think I'm too busy with fancier invites, so you'd be amazed at how often I sit alone at home," "Enjoy the climb up the ladder to success because there are very few rewards at the end. The fun is trying the climb," and (I love this), "If Nino ever really wants to find a nice girl, he should go to church and look there."

CHAPTER 10

Teach Me Tiger

In 1958, I had an idea for a song called "Teach Me Tommy." I told Nino, and he immediately sat at the piano. He changed "Tommy" to "Tiger" because Tommy was too personal and anyone could be called Tiger, and together we wrote "Teach Me Tiger." When we came to the part where I sang "wa, wa, wa, wa, wa," I was just filling in for the music, and then Nino recognized immediately that it was a great sound. He said to keep it and to use it whenever I could. We knew on the spot that we had a song—a really good commercial song!

I called Henri Rene. He wasn't at RCA as he had been years ago in the "I'm in Love Again" days. He was now the head of A&R (Artists and Repertoire) at Imperial Records, so Nino and I went up to his office to show it to him. Nino played piano, and I sang it. He wanted to record it right away, so in a few days, we went into the studio and cut it. After two or three cuts, we got a really good take. Nino said, "That's it! Just enough sex, but not overdone."

Henri thought I should do one more and push the sex a bit. Nino said, "Don't do it, Carol, or it will be banned." Unfortunately, I listened to Henri. We chose the last take, and it was banned. It made quite a bit of noise but just couldn't get the radio airplay it needed to be a hit record. Nino was usually right.

I recorded it in 1959, and today it is still being played and making money; checks come in regularly from all over the world. It is on our website and all over YouTube with all sorts of interpretations, and I get a lot of fan mail. The song was never a hit, but it is by far my most famous solo outing.

Many, many imitators have sung it in different countries and in different languages, and it is lip-synched by drag queens in clubs worldwide. A lot of people think Marilyn Monroe sang it. Not true! It has been on Animal Planet and on commercials all around the world. It's all so flattering. The thrill of all thrills in 1983: "Teach Me Tiger" was chosen by the astronauts on the *Challenger* space shuttle as the song they wanted to be awakened by their first morning in space. That really knocked me out! I was watching TV one night, and the news showed the astronauts in space, listening to my song! I could actually hear my record being played on the news on TV and see the astronauts, hearing my voice in space. I still get excited even now, writing it down.

I was invited to Edwards Air Force base to watch the astronauts' landing and meet them. I was thrilled. One of the astronauts came to our house in Northridge, California, for lunch. His name is Story Musgrave. Nino and I had so many questions to ask him. One was, "What was it like in space?" He said, "It was very dark like nighttime, *all* of the time." Next to winning the Grammy Award for "Deep Purple," I think this was my greatest thrill and achievement. How "Teach Me Tiger" just keeps rolling along after all of these years just amazes Nino and me.

I learned so much from Nino through our many years together. We both lived with our parents longer than we should have. I think if we had *had* to work—instead of having *chosen* to work—we would have been better off. In their big house, we wrote songs, sang, planned, and rehearsed together. I was not an easy study. Nino would think of the notes and harmonies, write them down, and then teach them to me. After Nino thought up the harmonies, I had to memorize them because I couldn't read music. I should have at least tried to learn, but I heard it was very difficult. So we struggled through until each song was perfect. (At least I had a good ear!) But it was very difficult for Nino since he was such a perfectionist and he had to work so hard with me. He also wrote the music for and had to rehearse with the band. Most of our success happened while we were living on Ingraham Street in Los Angeles. We would rehearse in the den, Nino sitting at the upright piano. I sat to the right of him on a wicker chair (which I still have). So many times, when I am sure I should have been listening to what he was saying to me, I would look at him and think, *God, he is so handsome with Mom's beautiful features and Dad's great chin—what a face!* No wonder all of my girlfriends had a crush on him.

He is truly a great talent and an exceptional tenor saxophonist, and with the people in the music industry, his name was always paired with his friend, Stan Getz. Had he not been so busy with *our* career, I'm certain he would have concentrated on his music and gone on to greater heights. People were always very stunned by the sound that came from Nino's saxophone—such warmth and feeling and sensuality. His heart goes so deep; you can't help but feel his music.

CHAPTER 11

Deep Purple

In 1961, Nino was hired to play saxophone on a recording session for Bobby Darin. Ahmet Ertegun from Atlantic Records was producing an album for him. During the session's time-off period, Nino played a song on the piano that he had written in the hopes that Bobby might like it. After the session, Ahmet went up to Nino and asked, "Hey what do you do besides play saxophone?" Nino said, "I write songs. My sister, April Stevens, and I are working on some songs, writing and harmonizing."

It didn't hurt that Ahmet happened to remember my voice and was a fan. He said he would love to hear what we were doing, so Nino invited him to our home on Ingraham Street in Los Angeles.

As long as I can remember, we have been singing together and harmonizing. Nino had been fooling around at the piano with some of the old standards we loved like "Sweet and Lovely" and "One Dozen Roses" and giving them a new sound and beat. I had heard that family members who sing together have a wonderful blend because their voices are similar. We were certainly family, and the sound that came out of our mouths in harmony was beautiful! We would both smile at each other with appreciation.

Ahmet said he would meet at our home at 4:30. It was almost 6:00 when he finally arrived. Mom was cooking her spaghetti and meatballs, and we usually ate at 6:30. We asked Ahmet if he would like to join us, and that began a habit he would continue for many years. Whenever he was in Los Angeles, he always saved one night to have dinner at our house. He too loved Mom's spaghetti and meatballs—especially her meatballs. He called them "those little round balls." In this book, I will be sure to include Mom's spaghetti and meatballs recipe exactly as she wrote it out for me.

When Ahmet heard our rendition of the old song "Sweet and Lovely" as Nino played it on the piano and we sang it with the harmony parts, he was very taken with it all and very interested in signing us to his recording company, Atlantic Records, and the subsidiary Atco Records.

Ahmet and his brother Nesuhi had come over from Turkey with their family when they were very young men. They loved music and contributed greatly to the jazz and rock and roll era. They made some powerful records.

Ahmet was such a colorful man. He was always an impressive dresser and was very attractive to the ladies. Very European.

He and Nino got to be buddies and spoke on the phone at least once a week. He always called when he was in Los Angeles, which was often. How they would laugh and carry on.

Ahmet was born in Istanbul, Turkey, in 1923. His father served as the first ambassador of the then-young Republic of Turkey to the United States. He and Nesuhi loved music and were the founders of Atlantic Records and known for discovering artists like Eric Clapton; Phil Collins; the Rolling Stones; Led Zeppelin; Crosby, Stills and Nash; Aretha Franklin; Ray Charles; the Drifters; the Coasters; and many more. Yes, we were in good hands.

Needless to say, that night he stayed for dinner and said he was interested in us. We were overjoyed—especially me! I couldn't believe my good luck, that maybe, just maybe, I would get another chance at singing and perhaps success. I certainly owed this to Nino.

One night, after recording at the studio in Hollywood, Nino, Ahmet, and Red Baldwin, one of the promoters, and I went to Martoni's Restaurant for dinner. It was a wonderful Italian restaurant and was frequented by many people in the music business. We sat at a small table at the bar, waiting for our table in the dining room.

Nino was looking at a pretty, young gal sitting at the bar. She had long, straight black hair and a very different-looking face. We said to him, "Ask her to sit with us if she'd like to." She did, and that was the beginning of his relationship with Cher. She and Nino dated for a while, and I asked him, "What is she like?" He said she was very nice and loved to go out dancing.

Nino brought her to the studio for a recording session and she met all our friends—Phil Spector, Sonny Bono, guitarists Tommy Tedesco and Glen Campbell. When Phil Spector needed girls' voices for background, she and I, along with the Blossoms, would fill in. We would always put Cher in the back since her voice was so loud. Shortly thereafter, she and Sonny Bono took off and made history together.

A few weeks later, we went in to the studio and cut the old standard "Sweet and Lovely." The Blossoms sang background for us. Darlene Love was one of the Blossoms at the time, and we were lucky to have her. They were all *great* singers, and they certainly enhanced the song!

The record was terrific and had a unique rock-and-roll sound. It was released, and we made appearances on all of the important radio shows in Los Angeles and outlying cities in San Francisco and wherever we could. It went to number five on the

West Coast, but we didn't get very much play in the rest of the country.

A few months later, we released the old standard "Paradise," and *again,* it only went up to number five on the West Coast—there just wasn't enough effort made to play it in the rest of the country. Many disc jockeys called our style "country Italian rock."

Next, we recorded and released a song that Nino and I wrote called "I Love Baby Weemus." It turned out to be number one in Canada, number one in Phoenix, and number one in France, so we knew we could sell records—if the disc jockeys would only play them. What should we do? Keep trying with Atco Records or go with another record company?

First, though, I must tell you how we happened to write "Baby Weemus." Nino had just written a song with the longest title ever put on a record label: "I've Been Carrying a Torch for You So Long That I Burned a Great Big Hole in My Heart."

In the bridge of the song is a line, "Baby *we mus'* part." I couldn't seem to get the harmony notes and remember them on that one line. We had to go over it so many times that soon we were saying "Baby Weemus." Finally, Nino, who was rehearsing me on the guitar, stopped playing and said, "What's a baby Weemus?" He began to strum his guitar very loudly as he sang, "I love Baby Weemus! Baby Weemus for me! Wee, wee Baby Weemus, she as fine as can be. I call her wee 'cause she's small. I call her baby 'cause she's my baby doll—wee, wee Baby Weemus, Baby Weemus for me." It happened that fast. We put harmony to it, and that was it.

When we recorded it, I sang the bridge of the song alone in a high-pitched baby voice. We hoped the song would be an interesting side and funny. "I Love Baby Weemus" was number one on the charts for record sales in Canada and Phoenix, Arizona. It was re-recorded in France and titled, "Jole Frimousse" and was on top of the charts there. One early evening, Nino was in the den, fooling around at the piano, as usual, and singing one of our favorite songs, the old standard "Deep Purple." We both loved the song, as most people did. He was playing it and singing and making fun of it, fooling around. We laughed and then looked at each other. It sounded good in our particular style. Were we crazy?

Dad was sitting in the adjoining room watching TV. When he came into the den, he said, "You know, I really liked that." We kept singing it, and he was dancing to it. He *never* did that, and when we came to the end of the song, where we sing, "And as long as my heart will beat, sweet lover we'll always meet, here in my deep purple dream," we all had tears in our eyes.

The song had chords in it that grabbed your heart and gave you shivers up and down your spine. It's called magic. Some songs had it, but many didn't. Usually the ones that did were hits. Don't ask me why. We humans feel things we cannot always explain.

A girlfriend of mine, Vickie Bascoy, came to our house at the time Nino and I were rehearsing "Deep Purple". She was always interested in our careers, so I asked her if she would like to hear what we were working on. She said, "Of course. You know I love your singing." So Nino sat at the piano, and we performed the song for her. When we came to the bridge of the song where Nino sang it alone (because it was in his key), he didn't know the words, so I softly whispered them to him just before he sang each phrase. She loved the song, especially the part where I spoke the words and Nino sang them, but I had a difficult time persuading Nino to let me speak them. But as Dad danced around the room, we just knew we really had a hold on to something big!

What a high that was! My God, what fun! We called Ahmet immediately and told him about the song. He was in Los Angeles in less than two weeks. We made plans for him to come to the house and hear the song and have dinner with us. He loved "Deep Purple" when he heard us sing it, and we went into the studio, where we had three hours to cut three songs!

We saved "Deep Purple" for last because the song didn't need all of the musicians and we could send some of them home. One of the musicians was Glen Campbell, who played guitar on many of our records before he became famous. Somehow, we only had fourteen minutes left to rehearse and record the song!

Nino quickly—and I mean quickly—talked it over with the guys in the band and Darlene Love and the girl singers, and we did it! Nino and I knew our parts well and just hoped there were not any clinkers! Holding our figurative breath, we got through it and played it back, and it still had the magic. We made it in fourteen minutes!

The sound could have been clearer, my voice could have been brought out louder on the harmony, and a few of the mechanical issues could have been perfected, but perfection doesn't make a hit record. *Magic* does. It's thrilling! It gives you chills! You love it. The movie *Gone with the Wind* had magic in it. Another song that comes to mind is "That Lovin' Feeling" or "MacArthur Park." We had it all in this record.

After the session, we were packing up when Glen Campbell came up to us to say good-bye. He said, "I never knew the two of you are brother and sister even after four years of knowing you."

Later that evening, we were home, playing the record a zillion times on the record player when Phil Spector called. He had heard us singing the song before we recorded it. While Nino was talking to him on the phone, I was playing it again on the record player. Phil said to Nino, "Nino that sounds like a hit record." He felt it on the other end of the phone.

Now Phil was not, by any means, the type of person to give compliments easily, so his comment really meant a lot to us.

Nino and Phil were good friends and had been for years. They both had a love of music in common, and they both loved to laugh and play tricks on each other. Phil also hired Nino to play saxophone on many of his records through the years. Around 1961, Phil and Nino wrote a song called "Why Can't a Boy and Girl Just Stay In Love?" I recorded it, but for some reason, it was never released.

Once, Nino and I had to go to New York City for a few days, and Phil said he would be there at the same time, staying at Jerry Leiber's (of the songwriters Leiber and Stoller fame) apartment and that we could stay there, too. It was a typical three-story brownstone with three or four bedrooms. We took him up on it.

One night while in New York City, the three of us went to see the movie *Psycho*. We laughed all the way home about how scary it was! The bedrooms in the apartment were on the third floor. Nino and Phil shared a large bedroom with twin beds. I was in a small bedroom down the hall. It had a huge clock above the bed like you would find on the outside of a building! Very strange and much too large for the room. But there it was, ticking away.

That night before I finally fell asleep, I could hear Nino and Phil talking and laughing for hours. In the middle of the night, something woke me up. In the darkness, I looked at the door and saw it being slowly pushed open. I screamed my lungs out! And then I heard a scream from the door at the same time and saw someone actually jump up in the air!

It was Phil, trying to push open the door to see what time it was. There wasn't another clock on the floor. We laughed for days at the way we both scared each other. I guess *Psycho* got to us! The last time I saw Phil, I mentioned it, and we still laughed.

Now back to "Deep Purple." Ahmet went back to New York City after we cut "Deep Purple," and he called Nino a few days later and said, "Hey, man, I played the record for everyone here, and they all said the same thing. It's the worst record you ever made." We could not believe it! What was going on? We knew the sound wasn't the best, but we had to make it so quickly! But all of the elements were there—the elements we loved! We were dumbfounded.

They were wrong, thank God, and we were right! One of the promoters at Atlantic Records in New York City, Jack Fine, said, "I love that record, and I'm going to make sure all of the disc jockeys I know play it because I know *if* it's played, it will be bought. People will buy it!" And he was right!

That was his mission, and he stuck to it. It was released in 1963. We put Nino's song, "I've Been Carrying a Torch for You So Long That I Burned a Great Big Hole in My Heart" on the back side, and it went to number one on the Billboard chart. The B side was the longest title ever put on the B side of a number one record. Before "Deep Purple's" release, we were known as April Stevens and Nino Tempo, (my name is first) then we decided to hopefully change our luck and put Nino's name first and go with Nino Tempo and April Stevens. That did it, a home run!

The first time I heard "Deep Purple" played on the radio, I was in the car on the freeway. I was so excited! I had to pull over and park on the ramp. What a thrill it was to hear it on the radio and know that so many other people were hearing it, too. Maybe in the next car! We did all that we could to help the record sell.

We appeared on *Bandstand* with Dick Clark three or four times. He was always wonderful and complimentary to us. We were on *The Lloyd Thaxton Show* many times, and he and Nino were very funny together, joking around. We went on *Shindig, The Smothers Brothers Show, Shivaree,* and *Where the Action Is.* There were a few people who said we ruined a beautiful song, but there were many more who absolutely loved it. I couldn't believe all this was happening to us.

We did many disc-jockey shows and record hops and interviews on radio. What a wonderful, busy time it was, living at home with Mom and Dad and seeing their joy at last! It was the best time ever. Phil Spector sent us a telegram saying, "'Deep Purple' is going to number one next week on *Billboard*. Congratulations. I'm happy for you both. Love, Phil."

CHAPTER 12

Grammy Award

When we were nominated for the Grammy Award, we were so proud. We didn't feel we would win, but who cared? We were nominated, and other fine records were nominated: Chet Atkins for "Teen Scene," Lesley Gore for "It's My Party," Little Peggy March for "I Will Follow Him," Ruby and the Romantics for "Our Day Will Come," and Sam Cooke for "Another Saturday Night"—all wonderful records! We really thought Sam Cooke would win the award.

We went to the Sixth Annual Grammy Awards on the night of May 12, 1964, held at the Beverly Hills Hilton Hotel. I wore a white, soft organza full short skirt with a black halter jersey top; a tight, black leather four-inch belt with a large rhinestone sunburst on the side; and black shoes. Nino had on a black suit. Nino had a date and I had a date, but we really didn't expect to be fortunate enough to win! We didn't even insist that Mom and Dad come with us because we didn't want to disappoint them. What a mistake that was!

We saw all of our friends and competitors there. Herb Alpert and Jerry Moss, owners of A&M Records were there as well as a few people from Atlantic Records, including Ahmet Ertegun of course. We sat at our table. Drinks and dinner were served while they announced the names of the winners. This was 1964, but the records and the winners were for the previous year. This was two years before the Grammys were televised, so it wasn't quite as big a deal as it is today.

They were just about to announce the best rock and roll record of 1963. I had just put some food in my mouth (naturally), and at that very moment, they announced *our* names! We just sat there, stunned. I was gulping and chewing and thinking perhaps my hearing was impaired, but the look on Nino's face said it all. He looked bewildered. His eyes opened so wide, and he began to stand. He moved toward the stage, with me right next to him. There was a thunderous applause! I couldn't believe the sound. It was so loud! The audience was so happy for us!

All we could think was, *We won! Why hadn't we insisted on Mom and Dad coming?* We thanked everyone onstage. Steve Allen and his wife, Audrey Meadows, were the presenters. We thanked the audience for all of their support and this great tribute. We were stunned!

Later, we were congratulated by all of our friends and peers—while we each looked for a phone to call to tell Mom and Dad the good news. They were so happy for us! *They* and only *they* were responsible for it all. We should have said that to the audience, but we really didn't expect to win and were so excited, we forgot. Damn it!

In March of the following year, 1965, I was asked to be a presenter at the Seventh Annual Grammy Awards at the Beverly Hilton. I was thrilled, of course, and Jimmy Durante was master of ceremonies. He was very nice, but not as funny as he was in television and the movies.

CHAPTER 13

Traveling

All of the traveling to Europe began. When we arrived in England, we learned we had to do a TV show in two hours. We had to get our bags off the plane, meet the people, and drive to the hotel. Before the trip, Nino told me to be sure to get the correct connector for my hairdryer because they were different in Europe.

When we arrived at the hotel, our rooms were next door to each other. I hurriedly rolled up my hair, took a shower, and then put the plastic cap on my head to dry my hair with the curlers on so I could do my makeup. I put my new connecter in the plug on the wall. I turned on the hairdryer and heard a *big* pop. All the lights went off in my room, and the end of my converter was smoking!

Immediately, there was a knock on my door. I opened it to a darkened hallway, and there stood Nino in his robe, saying, "What happened? All the lights went out."

He looked at me with the plastic cap on my head and the smoke coming from the converter and said, "Right on schedule, aren't you?" In spite of the mishap, the TV show went very well that night.

While recording for Atlantic Records (actually, we were on its subsidiary, Atco Records), we had more than a few hits in Europe. We traveled back and forth to England, Italy, Germany, and Holland, and the people and musicians there were wonderful. Great musicians! I don't know why, but that surprised us. We appeared on the most watched TV show in England called, "TOP of the POP "and sang "Deep Purple" and it was thrilling.

Another time when we arrived in Europe, the plane was late, so we had to go directly to the TV station to do a show in a matter of minutes. We didn't have time to even change clothes. Our luggage was momentarily lost anyway, so we just turned our T-shirts around and wore the clean sides. After all, it was the age of rock and roll, so the messier, the better!

When we were in Italy, we sang our songs that were popular there in Italian. If we were in Germany, we sang in German, and if we were in France, French. Nino was better at languages than I was, but we had teleprompters, so it wasn't so difficult. It was so much fun as I look back on it now.

Holland was wonderful! It was so different and unique. All of the homes had flowers perched on windowsills, and what a pretty sight it was. While we were there, we were asked if we could make an appearance in a circus going on at the time. Of course we said yes, never stopping to think just how we would be presented in a circus.

We walked into the arena with all of the circus acts and animals. They put us behind the elephants, naturally, and that was not too pleasant. Etta James, the famous singer of "At Last," was right there with us. What a joke it was, and how we all laughed.

While we were in Amsterdam, we went to the Rijksmuseum Museum and saw all of Van Gogh's paintings. It was so worthwhile. What a tragic life, and what beauty he painted.

We were invited to perform at the San Remo Festival on the Riviera. Frankie Laine, Paul Anka, and Ben E. King were among the performers. Don Costa was the orchestra arranger. I remember the photographers so well; they were everywhere, so aggressive and so many! Everyone wanted to take a picture.

Our records were a hit in Australia, too, so we were booked in Sydney at the Chevron Hotel. They had lovely rooms there for us and an international restaurant that featured a different chef every night from a different country, cooking and serving his or her particular food. It was free for the entertainers playing there. How lucky can you get? Nino and I had a ball—or should I say feast? One of us was—and usually both of us were—always in the restaurant.

Our show went really well there, except on Thursday nights. Dean Martin's TV show was on that night, and it was a huge success there, too. Everyone stayed at home to watch him. They certainly were not in our audience Thursday nights!

We also made friends with Dionne Warwick, who was appearing at the club across the street from the hotel. We got to see her show. She is a really nice gal and a great singer!

When we arrived in Australia, photos were taken of us at the airport for the newspaper the next day. On that particular day, I had on an extra-long, heavy gold chain around my neck with a solid gold medallion hanging on it. I was waving at the photographer, so you could clearly also see my heavy gold bracelet with a small gold watch dangling from it. They were both gifts from Glenn McCarthy and were very striking. I never should have been wearing them on a trip. Mom warned me not to take them with me.

The next evening, just before showtime, I ordered some light dinner to be sent up to my room. I just picked at it because I was hungry, but I didn't want to eat it all before the show, so I left a note for the maids that read, *Please do not take the food. Leave it. Thank you.*

After the show, I came back to my room and found that my two pieces of gold jewelry were gone. I think I just left them in a top drawer. They were absolutely gone! But my food was still there. Did I eat it? Yes. I was very sad, but I was also starving! At least the jewelry was insured, but certainly not for what it was worth, and it never was replaced. A good lesson to remember is not to take your good jewelry traveling—or to put it in the hotel safe.

About a month after winning the Grammy Award, Atlantic Records gave us a cocktail party at the Interlude Club on Sunset Boulevard in Los Angeles to celebrate our number one record on the Billboard charts. We took a lot of photos with Mom and Dad, Ahmet, his brother Nesuhi, and the rest of the men from Atlantic Records. There were at least a hundred people there. What a night that was. Cary Grant even came and sat with Mom and Dad at the table all night, and we were so proud he was there. He was such a special man.

Jayne Mansfield and her husband were there, and when I went up to her to introduce myself and say hello, she said, "I wouldn't have missed coming, April. Why, I copied my sexy style from your singing." Now *that* really surprised me, and I told her so. To this day, I don't know who invited them, but what she said to me certainly contributed to the happiness of the night. And believe me, Nino and I were bubbling over with joy, especially to see Mom looking so happy and beautiful and Dad with a big smile on his face all night. And, of course, Cary Grant, sitting right there with them. Soon after, we were on a flight to Seattle.

"Deep Purple" was a hit there, too, and we were booked to do some television shows. Nino said to me, "Now what do we do for a hit follow-up to 'Deep Purple'? It won't be so easy."

At that moment, there was music being played on the airplane. It was Muzak. The song was "Whispering," again an old standard, and I said, "How about this?" and pointed to where the music was coming from. We both smiled at each other and knew it was a perfect fit.

During the reign of "Deep Purple," we were booked into the Copacabana in New York City. While we were there, President Kennedy was killed in Dallas. What an unbelievable tragedy. Nino and I were devastated and hoped we didn't have to do a show that night. The owner, Mr. Jules Podell was sitting at the bar and Nino Whispered in his ear, "Mr. Podell, is it appropriate to sing tonight? Never even turning his head, he said," I'm paying you, you'll sing!" We did and we sang to 11 people in the audience. I don't know how we got through it. We were singing and crying at the same time, performing with a lump in our throats.

We recorded "Whispering" soon after "Deep Purple" began to come down on the charts. The song was a delight to sing. It went to number ten. It was such a natural song for harmony and sounded great to our ears, and our ears were not easy to please. Nino, as you know, was very particular about each note being right in tune, and I concentrated more on getting the feeling of the song. Together, we were a tough pair.

At that same sad time, the Beatles came to America. It was like a tornado hit! They were wonderful, and we loved their music. Everyone did! Their songs were fabulous and their voices and interpretations so different sounding. Everyone wanted Beatles records.

The recording artists here in America that were solid with many hit records behind them held on. But we were in a weak position, only having one hit record to our credit, and we didn't have a manager at that time, so we just seemed to flounder. I never did meet the Beatles, but in 1973, I met John Lennon at A&M Recording studios at A&M Records. He was there with Phil Spector and Nino. As I walked up to him, he turned and walked toward me, singing *my* harmony part to "Deep Purple." I was never so honored—that really shook me up! Then he said, "You must be the lovely April Stevens." It sounded even better with his English accent.

We recorded other records however, while at Atco. We sang the old song "Melancholy Baby" in our style. Then I sang "No Hair Sam" and "Morning 'Til Midnight." The latter was a song written by Bobbie Gentry, who had a big hit with her song "Ode to Billie Joe." Before her hit record, she came to our home in Los Angeles to play her new record that was to be released. It was called "Mississippi Delta." On the back side of the record was "Ode to Billie Joe." We heard both songs, and Nino told her that he liked the B side much better than the A side. "That's your hit," he said. She was surprised, but Nino was proven right. We also recorded "Lovin' Valentine" and the unreleased oldies "More Than You Know" and one of my favorite songs, "Memories of You." That song had magic, too, although it was also never released. (until now on Harkit Records)

We appeared every three months in either Harrah's Club in Reno, Las Vegas, or Lake Tahoe in the lounge, doing three or four shows a night. We felt our type of up-and-coming act should have been an opening act in the main room for a top performer, but when we finally found a manager, he didn't see it our way.

In 1965, we decided it was time to leave Atlantic Records and go with White Whale Records. Our relationship with Ahmet Ertegun from Atlantic Records never ceased. We were still the best of friends, and he and Nino were still very close. He still called whenever he came to Los Angeles, which was often.

We were doing a lot of rock shows around Los Angeles with the Beach Boys, the Righteous Brothers, and Sonny and Cher. In fact, Nino wrote a song especially for the Righteous Brothers called "All Strung Out," and although we were very good friends, they felt the song was too similar to what they had done in the past, like "You've Lost that Lovin' Feeling." I always felt they made a mistake, and so did Nino.

Finally, Nino and I recorded it. It came off beautifully and became a top ten record in whatever market it was played. But again, we didn't get enough play from enough areas. In Salt Lake City, it was number six, and it went to number twenty-six on the National Billboard, even with little airplay. We get more mail and comments even today on "All Strung Out" than practically any of our songs except "Teach Me Tiger." Just the other day, we got a comment on our website saying, *"All Strung Out" is the most "neo-spectorian" record ever.* So many compliments—this record really should have been a hit.

Around 1965, after the release of "All Strung Out," we got a letter from a Jim Chaffin from Salt Lake City. He was about fifteen years old, and his letter simply captivated me. I didn't have time to read it all, yet I couldn't put it down. It was so interesting, and he was so knowledgeable.

Today, forty-eight years later, he is still one of our closest friends. After corresponding for four or five years, we finally met in Reno when he and his parents and sister came to see us perform at Harrah's Club. Shortly after, he moved to and worked in Los Angeles for almost twenty years. We had a wonderful relationship then, too.

While we were recording, we could always count on Jim's opinion. No matter what, he would tell us the truth, even if it hurt—and it often did! He's been there for us for most of our careers, and although he now lives back in Salt Lake City, we are lucky to still have him in our lives, in charge of our website, www.ninoandapril.com. We still call him with all kinds of questions, and he always has the answers.

We talk often, and he sends Nino and me whatever our fans comment on. Lately, it's been all about our "All Strung Out" video and our appearance singing it on YouTube. What an unbelievable feeling it is to know people are enjoying your songs even today! That record got away from us and fell through the cracks, as a fan wrote. Anyway, Jim is the best friend, and we love him like family.

While we were with White Whale Records, we also recorded "You'll Be Needin' Me Baby," "My Old Flame," "The Habit of Lovin' You Baby" (which Nino wrote), and "I Can't Go On Livin' Baby Without You" (which Nino and I wrote.)

During the sixties, we worked in the lounges in either Reno or Vegas every three months. It was three or four shows a night and very hard work, but a lot of fun, too! On one particular day, I went to a beauty salon to have my hair done. This was unusual because I usually wore a fall or a wig because it was much easier to deal with. The hairstylist gave me a rather unusual hairdo, to say the least. It was much fluffier than usual, with more bangs, and strange looking for me. I wasn't too sure about it.

While we were dressing backstage, I said to Nino, "What do you think of my new hairdo?" He had something on his mind, I could tell, so he glanced at me and said, "It's fine—fine." I wasn't really satisfied with his answer because I knew his mind was somewhere else. So I waited, and then about ten minutes later I said, "Are you *sure* the new hairdo looks OK? Tell me!" He said, "April, you look great! I already told you!" So I figured it must look good.

Just as we were approaching the stage to go on, they announced, "And now Harrah's is proud to present Nino Tempo and April Stevens." At that very moment, my brother looked at me—*really* looked at me for the first time all evening—and said, "What in the world did you do to your hair?"

I was mortified! I don't have to tell you how I felt going onstage. I walked out trying to hide behind Nino. I knew I just had to make the best of it and forget my hair. But after the show, Nino heard from me, loud and clear! We have laughed about this for years!

Another night, the audience hadn't been as enthusiastic as usual. As we were coming offstage after the show, Nino looked at me in all seriousness (as only he can do) and said, "We had better get out of this business before they throw us out!" Exact words!

I started to laugh (wrong), and I said, "What are you talking about? This is a magical business. Some nights it's great, and some nights after doing the very same show, it's not up to par. Don't you think Sammy Davis has had similar shows?"

And with that, he looked at me with that same somber look on his face that always makes me laugh. I knew I had better start running, and he chased me back to our dressing rooms. By then, we were laughing. He was too serious, and I wasn't quite serious enough, but that's the way it was, and it never has changed.

We were appearing at one of the hotels in Las Vegas, and one afternoon after lunch, we saw Tony Bennett sitting at one of the tables. We knew him and thought we should talk to him. Maybe he could help us find the right manager. We were aware of the saying; "You need a manager behind you who has more talent than you have."

We said hello to Tony, and he asked us to sit down. Jerry Vale, who was also appearing in Vegas, sat down with us, and the first words that came out of his mouth were "Tony, you have to help me. I need a new manager." "You need one," Tony said. "I need one, too." With that, we looked at each other and left them alone with their heads together.

While playing the lounges in the sixties, we met Tina Turner. She is a very nice gal. She would come into my dressing room and say, "April, you are the only white chick I've ever seen that knows how to wear a wig!" That made me laugh because as I told her, "I just grab it, put it on my head, pin it down, and just barely run the comb through it." She said, "That's it. That's the secret! You can't try to get it too perfect. Mess it up a bit; then it won't look like a wig!" I guess I was doing something right.

Charo was also on the bill with us. She was always fun! She talked so fast, I could never understand her. She was married to the bandleader, Xavier Cugat. She sang hot and spicy Latin songs with a charming Spanish accent.

I did something right. I recorded "Wanting You," an old song that Nino arranged and produced. He had written an outstanding melody and tagged it on at the end. In my estimation, it is the best record, vocally, I have ever sung. I sang it alone, and for some unknown reason, whether it was the dance beat or the over-all feeling, my voice just jumped out of me, and it hit a range and volume that I didn't even know I was capable of. It really surprised the hell out of me! It has since become a big dance record in Europe. I'm sure if I had continued singing, my voice would have taken me in different directions. I really concentrated on it for a short amount of time and in such a small area—rock and roll and sexy songs.

A&M Records was newish and doing well with Herb Alpert and Jerry Moss at the reins. The Carpenters were beginning to bloom. We signed with A&M, and they were a fun company to be with. I was at the studio one day, looking for a phone booth to make a call, and there, in the phone booth, was Barbra Streisand. I am a huge fan of hers, and there she was, right before my eyes! I was so excited. I waited…and waited…and waited…for nearly half an hour for her to come out. But I didn't even mind waiting for her. Finally, she came out, apologizing profusely. "I am so sorry to take so long, but it was such an important call. I knew you were waiting a long time, but I had to finish it."

She was so beautiful. She had gorgeous skin and the prettiest blue eyes. She was a knockout. All I could say was, "Oh, that's OK," and smile. She was so nice in person, and I didn't expect that. What a day, and what a lovely surprise.

I believe the first song we cut for A&M Records was "Love Story," and it was a hit in the Netherlands, so off we went to Holland to do some television. We loved it there. Then we did "You Turn Me On" and "Put It Where You Want," and then Nino and composer, producer, and songwriter Jeff Barry cut a sax album called *Come See Me Round Midnight*. Nino's group was called, "5th Ave. Sax." I was at the studio while they were cutting an instrumental called "Safari." I was sitting there and wrote a lyric to the melody and called it "Wake Up and Love Me." It's about a girl who falls in love with a younger man. He's asleep, and she's trying to wake him up.

Nonno and Nonna after they were married and she is pregnant with my Mom.

I was three years old and had trouble putting my bathing suit on. The beginning of doing things backwards.

Nino and me as children in front of Nonnu's saloon and Grill, Dad's grocery store on corner.

Mom and Dad shortly after they were married.

My Grandparents and their seven daughters. Left to Right, Sarah, Nonno, Nonna, Nini, Mom, Francis, Isabel (who sewed my gowns) Elaine (who helped me so much.) and Donnie.

Winning the Radio station KLAC singing contest in 1946. Left to right, Lucile Ball, "Mary", (who I shared the winnings with), Al Jarvis, the D.J., Me, Charles Bickford and Desi Arnaz.

Leigh Sterling, Nino and me entertaining at the veteran hospital in Los Angeles every Monday night.

- A couple of sailors and Me.

Singing at the famous Hollywood Canteen in 1945. I was still Carol Lo Tempio.

Eddie Fisher and April back stage.

Liberace with me and Seymour Heller's (our Manager) and his wife at a club with a D.J..

Singing, "I'm in Love Again" for the Marines at Camp Pendleton in Oceanside, California.

Glenn McCarthy and I with John Carroll and friends having dinner in Las Vegas.

__Humphrey Bogart and me in the same photo! What a trip! It was taken at the Shamrock Hotel's Emerald Room. 1952__

Cary Grant and Dyan Cannon at our home in Los Angeles enjoying Mom's Spaghetti dinner. It happened often.

Nino and Me receiving the Grammy Award. 1964. It was an unbelievable evening.

At a party given by Atlantic records for "Deep Purple's" success. Mom, Dad, Cary Grant, Ahmet Ertegun and friend.

Mom, Dad, Nino and me with our gold record of "Deep Purple". What a Prize.

Nino and Me with the Righteous brothers on tour.

Sonny, Cher, Nino and Me

Publicity photo with me, saxaphone and Nino.

Nino, Bobby Darin, Sandra Dee, me

My "Cabo Man", Bill with Sheldon in front of his home in Cabo San Lucas, 1984

Wedding day at Mom's home in Northridge, California. 1985

My new family. Starting left to right in back row, Blake, Garrett, Justin, Michael, Gary, Julie, Bill and Laura. Middle Row, Bob, Erin, Lisa, Madison, Bree and me. Front Row, Macee and Nicole.

Traveling

April with the Masai natives in Kenya, Africa, I am the one in the middle. I was goofy!

April being inducted into the Buffalo Music Hall of Fame, 1999

Bill and I celebrating my Birthday recently at Melvyn's in Palm Springs, California

CHAPTER 14

Righteous Brothers

In 1969, Bill Medley and Bob Hatfield of the Righteous Brothers asked Nino and me to go on tour with them. Also on board were the Blossoms, three great backup singers including the talented vocalist Darlene Love. They sang on "Deep Purple" and on many of our hit recordings. They also had many hits on their own as Darlene Love and the Blossoms.

We played throughout the Midwest, doing six weeks of one-nighters with eleven days off. We traveled by plane if the distance was far, but mostly we went by car and bus. It was quite an entourage, with Bill and Bob and their band consisting of about six musicians, the soundman, the manager, and all of the equipment.

What a load it was, and what fun and laughs we had. We played colleges and stadiums, and the crowds were immense and wonderful. The Brothers had a great musical and comedy act. Although I heard it every night, I laughed every night. Darlene Love and the Blossoms were powerful.

Nino and I did a medley of our hit songs for about twenty minutes. Then Nino played a medley of Burt Bacharach hits on the saxophone and brought down the house! It is strange because our good friend and pianist, Andy Thomas, arranged the songs, and Nino was sure it wouldn't work. To his amazement, the audiences loved it, and it brought the loudest applause. We did the same medley in our regular act. We just shortened it. We usually sang many of the hits of the day, also.

I did a ballad, and then I sang "Teach Me Tiger." Each night, I picked a young man from the audience to come up on the stage. I put his arm around my waist and sang it to him. The poor darlings, they just about passed out. I would have, too, if that had been done to me, but I kept it in the act because it was so funny and got so many laughs.

We closed with "All Strung Out," and the reaction to the song really surprised us. We had no idea it was so popular. One night after our show, Nino asked me, "Is the applause as great as I think it is after we do 'All Strung Out'?" The song should have been a hit because whenever it was played on the air, it was loved! Even now, we constantly get fan letters and comments on YouTube about it. Here is a comment from August 2011: *Nino Tempo and April Stevens totally captured my heart and soul with this magnificent song and performance on "All Strung Out," the ultimate in harmonic beauty, one of my top ten favorites ever!"*

One fan wrote this to us after watching us perform " All Strung Out" on the Lloyd Thaxton show, "*Gosh, Nino Tempo and April Stevens always sounded so good together, so talented. This team has it all. Lloyd knows great music. What a rush! Many thanks for this.*" Our web manager, Jim Chaffin, sends the comments to us, and we usually send a thank-you back. A usual day on the road with the Righteous Brothers began at 6:30 a.m.: breakfast in the motel or hotel, back to the room to pack up, and a four- or five-hour car trip to our next job. We took a plane only if the miles were long and we had the day off. We stopped for lunch and then went to a hotel close to the stadium or college where we were performing. We had four or five rental cars and an SUV for the instruments and sound equipment. Upon arrival, the soundman would immediately go to the stage area and set up the sound system for the night. The performers would get food and unpack and rest until showtime.

We liked to travel by bus or plane so we could all be together. Bill, Bob, and Nino were especially witty. They would tease each other unmercifully about the funny things that occurred. My jaw hurt every night from laughing so much. It was a wonderful experience.

CHAPTER 15

The Seventies

After years of inactivity, in 1979, we decided to do a performance at the Back Lot Theatre in Los Angeles for four nights. We booked ourselves at the theater because we wanted to invite a few agents to come and see our show in hopes that they would book us.

They didn't show up—not one of them. It was heartbreaking. We had worked for a month renewing the songs and show. Our family and friends were all there, but no agents.

If our dear friends, Jim Chaffin and Bob Gibbons, had not had our show videotaped, we would not have a copy of it today. The film isn't the clearest or the sound the best, but thanks to them, we at least have a video of our act.

One day, while in a restaurant in Hollywood, I happened to spot Robert Goulet sitting alone. It was very unlike me, but I always liked his singing and I thought I would tell him. Before I could say anything other than my name, he said, "Oh, I've been a fan of yours for so long. I used to be a disc jockey, and I played all of your records." It was a surprise for both of us. He looked more handsome than in pictures.

In 1974, I had an idea for a song. Nino was the true songwriter of the family, but he did like what I wrote. He helped me write it, and then we showed it to Phil Spector, who added some of his magical thoughts to it. It was called "A Woman's Story," a sad lament of a woman who is passed around and who has finally found true love and really needs this love.

It was recorded in 1975 by Cher with Phil Spector's Wall of Sound Orchestra on the Warner-Spector label with a tremendous amount of publicity. Can you imagine how excited I was? Cher and Phil Spector together with the Wall of Sound Orchestra. It was, I'm sorry, to say, an unsuccessful effort; I always felt it was done too slowly. It should have been more like Cher's record of "Gypsies, Tramps, and Thieves." I recorded it shortly after, and changed it somewhat. Nino helped me make a demo, but we elected not to release it. We called it "I Found My Man." Then in March 1986, a singer by the name of Marc Almond recorded "A Woman's Story," which can be heard on YouTube and it is a great recording.

Love Kills is a book that Dan Greenberg wrote in 1978. A friend called me and said, "April, you are in this book I'm reading." I said, "You're kidding. What is it?" She told me, and I picked it up in the bookstore. Sure enough, I was in it. It was a murder mystery about a serial killer who kills all women the exact same way—in his home with one of my records playing. The record was *"Teach Me Tonight"*, which I never recorded. I think the author meant my recording of *"Teach Me Tiger"*. The book was supposed to have been made into a movie, but it didn't happen.

I did speak to Dan Greenberg and told him that he got the title of the song wrong. He apologized, and I said it was OK and that at least he got my name right, and we laughed.

In 1977, I had a partial hysterectomy. I was home recuperating when I got a phone call from Nino saying, "I just got a call from the Sahara Hotel in Late Tahoe. They want us to fill in for Kenny Rankin for a week starting in two days. He is appearing with Flip Wilson in the big room with Don Costa's orchestra. There was a problem with something off-color that Kenny said to the audience, and the bosses are angry and want to replace him with us."

He added, "I know you have only been home for a few days since your operation, so if you don't feel you can make, it's OK. They will understand."

I had been lying down and walking slowly, favoring my stomach. But when Nino said those words, I immediately stood up straight as an arrow and said, "I'm just fine. When do we start?"

It was a wonderful, fulfilling engagement. We were finally in the big room with a magnificent orchestra, and the difference was tremendous. We ended each performance with Jimmy Webb's hit song "MacArthur Park" and got a standing ovation! What a joy it was for us. What a feeling to see the audience standing and smiling and applauding us.

One night, two of Nino's business friends, Ronan Gomberg and Sheldon Pollack, were in the audience. After the performance, they came backstage and raved about the show, especially "MacArthur Park." They knew we didn't have a recording company at the time, and they wanted to give us money as an investment to record the song. They were impressed with our version of the beautiful song, and we more than did it justice. The standing crowd brought tears to my eyes every night. We turned down our friends because we were afraid to take their money and take a chance with it. It was the wrong thing to do. We now feel it would have been a great career move for us and a great financial move for all of us. We sang this arrangement of "Mac Arthur Park" at the "Back Lot Theatre" and the video of us performing it can be seen on You Tube.

In 1979, I was still living at home, and Dad was ill with prostate cancer. It was at a time when people were not very diligent about seeing doctors regularly. It all lay very heavy on us.

We were living in Northridge in a beautiful two-story home. Nino had an apartment in Beverly Hills, but he seemed to be at home with us most of the time. We were not working, and everything seemed to have stopped for a few years.

CHAPTER 16

Home in Los Angeles

Mom was after me about going into the Little Club to sing. It was a popular small entertainment room in Beverley Hills with a show business clientele. "Even with just a pianist behind you, I know you will capture them," she said. Oh, what confidence she had, and, oh, how I wished I would have listened to her, but I was so used to singing with Nino that the thought of standing up there alone, singing for an hour, frightened me. The same old insecurities engulfed me.

During that time, I was dating Bruce Hayes. I was very fond of him. He was a very attractive and intellectual divorced father of two beautiful little blonde daughters. He did voiceovers and commercials on TV. He was a dreamer and not realistic about the future and as the romance lingered on I realized that the relationship would have not worked out.

The Carloses, our neighbors, lived next door to us in Northridge. Angela was from Taiwan, and Dante was from the Philippines. They were in their early thirties and were lovely people. She had time on her hands and wanted to open a small children's boutique in Encino called Cute Marie's. She wanted me to help her while she got it started, and then later she would get someone permanently.

At first I said no, and then I thought about it. To work for a few hours, two or three days a week, was not a bad idea. So I did help her, and then at night, I'd come home and tell my mom and dad all about my new experiences.

After we opened, I had to deal with the cash register. I just couldn't make change fast enough, and the whole process made me nervous. I prayed that no one would come in and buy anything. If I sold something, having to make change was overwhelming for me. It was a joke. We all laughed, but I did it for about six months.

In the meantime, I had a friend, Vern Langdon. He was an entertainer, a songwriter, and a fan of mine. He used to live in the San Francisco area and was a disc jockey on a small radio station. He played all of my records, even the sexy "Teach Me Tiger." How brave he was!

By that time, he had lived in Los Angeles for many years. We became close friends. One night, he and his wife and I were in a restaurant, and I spotted Mae West. Vern knew her very well and wanted me to meet her. I was nervous to meet the *forever*-popular Mae West. I put out my hand when Vern introduced us, and she said, "Gosh, I love your 'Teach Me Tiger.'" What a surprise!

Vern cut an album in 1981 with a large orchestra. His dream was to sing, and he did just that. He sang his own compositions, and they were good songs; they just weren't commercial. He was not happy with the result since he was not a singer but had always wanted to be. The realization was not a happy one, and he called to tell me the story. He wondered if I would be interested in trying to see if the songs were in my key. He was interested in putting my voice on the album.

I agreed, but I really didn't think the songs would be in my range. I was wrong. I was able to sing them, and I really liked the songs. They came out beautifully. Although it's not a commercial album, it is called *Carousel Dreams* on the USA record label. Vern has since passed on, and I miss him very much because we were always in touch.

CHAPTER 17

Dad

I get very emotional when I think of my dad. He was my soft spot. We had a connection, though we never spoke of it, and I never kissed or hugged him as I should have. But I know he knew. Somehow we were all so shy at that time.

It is so different today; we kiss so easily. We never really showed much affection unless we were going away or returning or on holidays or birthdays. But you could see it in our eyes that we adored each other and could not do enough to please each other.

I see my dad in my mind when he came home from work, standing in the doorway with his arms full of bags of food for us. He either owned a grocery store in the early years or worked for someone who owned a grocery store. All of his life, he worked and carried groceries to us. He was my hero, and I know he protects me and watches over me even today. I can feel him.

Thoughts of him hit me so deeply. One day when he was ill, he was sitting in the front room in his chair, and I was standing by him. He took my hand and kissed it and then held it. I know so well what he was saying to me.

Soon, he was in the hospital, and when he passed on, that very night, December 1, 1981, I had a dream that Nino and I were small children, and we were asleep in our twin beds, and Dad came in through the window and kissed us both good-bye and then left, fading out of the window.

It was so real, I felt it really happened. I saw him and felt him. Up to that time, I had never had anyone that close to me die, and for it to be him was unbearable for the three of us. We had all been so unusually close for so many years. But that is the way our life happened, and I wouldn't have it any other way. I cherish every day we had.

We missed him terribly, and I could never ever get over what a total disappearing act death is. That is what struck me. They are gone from us. They just disappear forever and always. Dear God, it's a bad plan. Why did you make it is so hurtful?

Just the thought of him was painful. Tears just poured out of me. And now as the years go by, I find a peacefulness just thinking about him and letting him in.

CHAPTER 18

Bill

I continued to help Angela in her shop but planned to leave shortly. Also, I knew I had to finalize the situation with Bruce, the man I had been seeing, and I dreaded facing it. So much time had gone by, and I now knew it would never work. Most of my life, I've avoided confrontations, but I knew I would have to do it.

I was at the shop one day when I got a phone call from Nino. He said Lennie Poncher had called him. Lennie was a very successful businessman in the automotive and housewares industry who we knew. He was also very prominent in the music and entertainment industry. Doing both was very unusual, but then, Lennie was a very unusual guy. He loved music and entertainers, and in the sixties and seventies, he managed the careers of Dianne Carroll, Leslie Uggams, Tito Puente, Jan and Dean, and many others. He was asked to go to England once to see a musical group and perhaps sign them, but he didn't like what he saw and heard. They just didn't have it, he thought. They were called the Beatles.

Late in January 1983, Lennie called Nino to ask him to if he could play his saxophone at a show to introduce a new line of stereo speakers and also to ask if he would come to dinner at Angie's

Restaurant in Santa Monica that Friday night so they could talk about it. Then he said, "Ask April if she would like to come along for dinner. My wife and another couple will be there."

Nino asked me if I would like to go, hoping I would say no as he would have to drive from Hollywood to Northridge to pick me up and was afraid I would not be on time. I said that I'd love to go. Lennie was always so funny, and I knew it would be a fun night.

On the way to the dinner, Nino asked me if I had made any decisions about Bruce. I told him that the relationship, as far as I was concerned, was not working. Nino advised me to tell Bruce soon because these things are hard enough without prolonging them. I said, "I plan to tell him tomorrow." And that was true. Those were my exact words, and it seemed like they went from my mouth to God's ears because of what happened next.

We arrived at the restaurant early, as Nino is always punctual. We elected to stand rather than sit down right away, and then Lennie walked in with three men and a woman. He walked up to us and introduced us to the man and his wife and then to Bill Perman and his son, Gary Perman. Why were the Permans there? I'll tell you later. Lennie introduced us as April Stevens and her brother, Nino Tempo.

While we were being introduced and still standing, Bill Perman said to me, "I like your name," and I said, "So do I." He was very attractive. He wore sunglasses, a T-shirt, jeans, a leather jacket, and cowboy boots. He had rather curly, dark brown hair and a small mustache. I couldn't see his eyes because of the sunglasses, but I liked what I could see of his face. He was about five feet, eleven inches tall and in his early fifties. He made sure to sit on my left. Nino was on my right, and aside from saying hello to Lennie's wife when she came to the table after a few minutes had gone by, I don't remember talking to anyone else but Bill all evening.

It seemed as though Bill Perman and I had a lot to say to each other. I had lost my father a year before, and Bill had lost his wife. At one point in the evening, Nino kicked me under the table as if to say, "Why aren't you talking with anyone else?" I kicked him right back.

Bill was in bad shape since his wife of eighteen years, Nora, had passed away a few months before in Cabo San Lucas, Mexico, where they had been living for the past two years. She had an aneurysm that burst one afternoon while lying on the beach. They were in the midst of her mother's eightieth birthday fiesta at their new waterfront home. Both of their families and loads of their friends were in Cabo, and the fiesta went on from Christmas to New Year's.

On January 2, 1983, Bill was out fishing, and Nora was lying on the beach when she complained to a girlfriend that she had the most awful headache she had ever had. She had been prone to headaches now and then, but never like this one. She went into a coma and had to be driven to the airport in the back of a truck and then was evacuated by air to a hospital in La Paz and then on to San Diego.

The whole family went to the hospital, but she never regained consciousness. Everyone was devastated.

Bill and Nora had a wonderful, loving marriage, and he had helped raise her son, Michael, who was six years old when they married.

Nora was very much loved by everyone who met her, especially in Cabo San Lucas, where she spoke the language and was able to help many of the ex patriots with various local problems. Then out of nowhere, this catastrophe happened. Everyone was blindsided. After a couple of months, Bill said he just had to get away, so he visited his son, Bob, in Manhattan Beach for a few days for a change of scenery. Then he went to visit with his youngest son, Gary, and his family in the San Fernando Valley.

Gary had been working for Lennie Poncher for about five years. Bill was an ex-partner of Lennie's. He had an office in Northern California and then decided to retire at the early age of forty-five. Lennie thought Bill was out of his mind to stop working when he was at the top of his game, but there was no changing Bill's mind. He and Nora bought a diesel trawler and sailed and lived on the boat for two years. With his two sons and Gary's fiancée, Suzanne, they cruised all over Mexico and the Sea of Cortez. When Bill and Nora saw Cabo San Lucas, they fell in love with it, sold the boat, bought a condo, and later bought a beautiful house on the ocean. I never even heard of Cabo San Lucas before that evening.

After he told me his story, he said, "Let's get on a lighter subject" as he finally took his sunglasses off. I know he had forgotten they were on, and yes, he had light green eyes. I was a goner!

He asked, "What do you do?" I told him, and although he loved music, he had never heard of Nino and me. He said his only claim to rock and roll fame was being a good friend of Keith Richards and his wife, Patti, since they lived in Cabo and were his neighbors. I said, "I can't top the Rolling Stones."

Then he told me a funny story. When Keith Richards got married in Cabo, Mick Jagger flew in for the occasion. They were all at Keith's bachelor party, having a rip-roaring good time, when Keith and Mick went over to the upright piano and began playing and singing "Somewhere Over the Rainbow." Feeling no pain, Bill went up to them, put his arms around them, and joined in the song. Mick looked at Bill and then at Keith and said, "Who the fuck is this guy?" I didn't know Bill at the time, but now that I do—that is *so* Bill.

Then he said, "I could hardly believe that tonight of all nights and of all the restaurants in Los Angeles, we picked Angie's, the same restaurant where you and Lennie were having dinner. I was at the office all day, and Lennie was encouraging Gary and me to have dinner with him and his friends. We declined because we haven't had any time alone together, so later, after deciding to come here, we were in the lounge, sitting at the bar talking and waiting for a table when who walks in but Lennie—and here we are!" Lennie Poncher is very persuasive.

I liked Bill Perman. He was a very attractive, friendly, and warm man. Even with all of his problems, he consoled me about losing my dad a year earlier.

He had much to say about everything. He was very interesting and smart. He got it! Whether it was a joke, a story, or just an indication, he got it immediately. I liked that.

After dinner, Gary got up from the table and said, "Dad, I'm going to leave. You have a car, so just come to the house when you're ready." They hugged and kissed, and I thought that was nice to see. I was impressed because at that time, people rarely embraced—especially men.

We talked awhile longer, and I hoped that he would ask for my phone number, but I didn't think he was ready for a move like that. Just then, Nino said that we had better be going, so we stood up, and Bill said, "I'm going to Northern California tomorrow to visit family and friends, but I'll be back soon, and I'd like to call you and see you again." I smiled as I wrote my phone number, and I looked up at him and said, "What was your name again?" Can you imagine!

As soon as Nino and I were alone in the car, he said, "What on earth were you doing?" I said, "I met *the* man!" Those were my exact words. I had never said them before. Nino just looked at me, amazed, and asked, "Do you mean the man you were talking to all night? You're kidding!" But I knew he was the one and that Mom was right.

As soon as I got home, I ran upstairs to Mom's bedroom and told her that I had met *the* man. She was in bed and turned so fast that she almost fell out. I laughed and said that I had that feeling and that it was just like she said it could happen.

The next morning, when I answered the phone at Cute Maria's, it was Bill. He said he changed his plans and asked if I would like to go to dinner the next night. I said that I would. He must have felt something, too. My aunt Elaine and her husband, Dom, had moved to Los Angeles, and she was helping me at the store with the cash register. When I got off the phone, she laughed at me because I was so flustered and stuttering.

When our doorbell rang the next evening, Mom answered the door and introduced herself to Bill. He looked at her and said, "Wow. I don't know who I should be taking out tonight—April or you!" We all laughed, and then Bill and I went to a Chinese restaurant in Northridge called Plums.

It had a lovely ambience, but halfway through the dinner, Bill excused himself and was gone from the table for about ten minutes. I began to wonder if he had left or that perhaps something was wrong. When I looked up, he was standing there with tissues stuffed in both nostrils. He explained that he had been having nosebleeds lately. He said, "Please bear with me and excuse my look for the evening."

He looked so comical with those tissues sticking out of his nose that we laughed ourselves silly. After fifteen minutes, he was back to normal, but I shall never forget our first date. It was memorable!

He then invited me to his son's home in Tarzana, and I met Gary's wife, Suzanne, and two-year-old son, Justin. Naturally, I found out more about Bill.

He first married his high school sweetheart when he was eighteen in Oakland, California. He had a daughter, Laura, then a son, Bobby, and then Gary. Bill was in the maritime service for two years. The marriage lasted for eighteen years. He then met

Nora and had a wonderful eighteen years with her, and I am certain it would have continued if she hadn't passed on.

He then set up a dinner party at the Black Whale Restaurant in Marina Del Ray. The restaurant was owned by Nora's niece, Michelle, and her husband. The family and quite a few of his friends were there. I met Bob, his oldest son, and Michael, Nora's son, and Michael's wife, Lisa. They were all wonderful to me although I was a bit nervous.

Bill was leaving for Cabo the next day. He said he and a group of men had planned a ten-day trip, cruising the coast of Mexico on a sixty-foot sport fisherman yacht. He promised to write me often, and he said perhaps when he returned, I might be able to come to Cabo to visit.

That night when we arrived in front of my house in the car, he kissed me, and I really liked kissing him. I could tell he knew his way around women by the way he held me. Real close! He was very confident.

While Bill was away, he wrote me every night and then mailed the letters at the first port. I was so happy to see his letters in the mail. The fact that he kept his word was most important. He told me practically everything he was doing. I felt that he needed this trip.

Bill soon came back to LA, and it was wonderful to see him. He told me that he had decided to go back to work with Lennie and Gary in Los Angeles. The news was music to my ears.

I then invited Bill to our home for dinner. It was just the four of us—Nino, Bill, Mom (the cook), and me. It was fun, and the food was delicious, but Bill had a little too much to drink. The more he drank, the more he talked, and he said, among other things, that he had become a "vagabundo" while living in Cabo. He gave the impression that he was just a beachcomber.

I knew it wasn't true. I knew he had a very prosperous sport fishing business with his brother-in-law in Cabo, and Nora had been their secretary. They were very successful.

Right in the middle of this dinner conversation, Nino excused himself and went to the downstairs bedroom. He called the kitchen phone, knowing I would pick it up. He said, "Don't let on that it's me. Can you come in here for a minute?"

I excused myself and went into the bedroom. Nino asked, "Did you hear what he just said? He's a vagabond. This is the man that you think is so special and wonderful?" I couldn't help but find the situation—that of Nino calling me on the phone—amusing. However, I didn't dare laugh. I said, "It's all the drinks he had, Nino. He's been through so very much lately. I know this man. He wrote to me every night he was away. I can't blame you for thinking otherwise tonight, but please don't worry."

Later that evening, I told Bill that the impression he made with his drinking and the things he said to my mother and brother didn't "go over." I spared him nothing. But I also added that I understood his point of view and what he meant. He had been through horrific and terrible things. I told him how sorry I was. I also said that no one in my family drank, so I wanted him to be careful.

He took all of it very seriously. He knew that he had had too much to drink and had been wrong, but I also noticed a tiny smile somewhere on his face—like he kind of admired the way I handled it. He apologized. I really liked this man.

Soon, Bill left for Cabo again. He asked me to join him, and I told him I would think about it. I spoke to Mom, and she said, "Carol, I know how you feel about Bill, but I do think you two should wait before you go to Cabo to visit. His wife was very popular and loved there, and not enough time has gone by for you to make that trip."

I said, "But he wouldn't have asked me if that were the situation. He wouldn't want me to be uncomfortable there."

She insisted that Bill didn't know quite what he was doing, that he was all mixed up, and that it was not unusual in his situation. She advised me to wait a few months before I went to visit.

I talked it over with Bill when he called, and he said it was quiet there and he was lonely, and he wanted me to come down and to be sure to bring my new album, *Carousel Dreams*.

I gave it some thought, and a few weeks after he left, I flew down to meet him. I was so excited when I left, and then about halfway through the flight, I felt like a truck ran me over. I wondered what I was doing and why I was going there so soon. Part of Nora's family was there. Bill said they were OK with my coming, but what if they weren't? Mom was right again. It was too soon.

Then I got scared and realized that he must be feeling just as I was. It was too strong with me for him not to feel the same way. If he weren't there to meet me, I would quietly get back on the plane.

But he was there, with his sunglasses on, a pair of khaki shorts (his legs were great!), and a vest. Sheldon, a sweet ten-pound terrier, was on a leash. Bill looked like Errol Flynn. Help! But as soon as we started talking, he was just my Bill.

He even admitted, as strange as it may seem, that he too felt a little apprehension about his asking me to come there so soon. I knew it! But we were so happy to be together again. There were a few times when I felt a tiny bit uncomfortable, like when he introduced me to the maid as his *sobrina* (cousin). She looked at me suspiciously, but all in all, I had a wonderful time.

I met some of Nora's family and friends and loved them. I also fell in love with Sheldon, the little white terrier. He was somewhat confused with my presence, but he wasn't the only one.

I also fell in love with Mexico, the people, the music, and the food. It turned out to be a great trip, and whatever Bill and I did wrong at the time, it all turned out to be beautiful. We were destined to be together.

Bill's home was absolutely beautiful. There were three bedrooms in a two-story house. It was all tile, and the stairway was very wide and very shallow, making it so easy to go up and down.

We were on the back deck, not far from the ocean and the famous Cabo San Lucas arches, lying on a lounge talking and laughing and going over many popular songs from the past. He really surprised me with his knowledge of all the lyrics. He knew them all! The only light was from the stars, and shooting stars were in abundance that night. He lit some candles in a few places. Later, with my new album and my voice floating around in the background, he really didn't have a chance.

Then, back in LA, we dated often and got very serious. We went back and forth to Cabo, and Bill leased the house, and we stayed at a lovely condo that he also owned there. We usually drove to Cabo and had a great time. Sheldon and I would race to the truck every morning, trying to outrun each other to sit next to Bill. Sheldon usually won.

I loved driving there because the topography was so unusual. It was either huge boulders of all sizes or black volcanic area. Other areas were absolutely covered as far as you could see with cactus! And then we would drive along and come to a lush area with palm trees and everything tropical. There was no in between. It was most unusual and enchanting. This place was Mulegé, Baja Sur. The *posadas* (hotels) were lovely and made of beautiful Mexican tile and so unusual looking.

We returned to LA, and Bill said he would soon be working there. He would have to get a condo, and he asked if I would consider living with him for about a year and then we would marry. He knew I had never lived with any man before. Even all the years with Glenn—the longest I had ever spent with him was ten days. I knew Bill needed that year, so I talked it over with Mom. She didn't like it, but of course, I was way over the age of consent.

We found a lovely condo in Westwood, and life was glorious. I cooked (I tried to remember what Mom did), and I kept the house clean, but I just couldn't get the hang of how to use the washing machine. I really tried. I took care of Sheldon and drove out to see Mom in Northridge every other day.

On many weekends, we drove to Lennie and Pattie Poncher's house in Palm Springs. Other friends of theirs were invited, too, and it was such fun. Lennie was the little matchmaker and cook.

Through the years, when I was at a party or a club, I was always asked to sing, which was natural. But what was not natural is that I never could and never did! I have always said I was too shy, and that is the truth. Also, I didn't want to disappoint them and not having rehearsed, I didn't know what to sing. Most of my songs are highly stylized, and the hits I had with Nino, I sang the harmony part. To just sing any lovely song, I didn't know what key to sing it in. I wish I could have been like Vickie Carr. She could jump up and sing any song whenever asked and come off great! (By the way, she also came to pasta dinner at our home.) I guess it all boils down to my shyness and not wanting to disappoint anyone, but I always hated to turn people down, especially my husband. (He does hear me sing in the shower, though.)

One day, Bill took me to San Pedro to Nora's family home. I met her mother and her sisters and part of the family. The whole family would add up to about one hundred people. They were wonderful and made me feel so at home. They reminded me of my family in Niagara Falls with all the warmth and love and laughter. I was in the kitchen with Nora's mother, and she pointed to Bill in the other room and said, "He is still my favorite son-in-law."

I even dreamed of Nora one night. I dreamed she came to visit us, and she and I were cooking for Bill in the kitchen and laughing and getting along great, and then in my dream, I began to wonder *who* was going to sleep with Bill that night. Good question. That sure woke me up fast!

I told Bill. At first he just looked at me, speechless—then he chuckled. Naturally! A family friend of his said to me, "You'll never be bored with Bill Perman." Truer words were never spoken. He is quite a guy, and so very funny. He calls me Tinkerbell. I asked him why he calls me that and he said, " There is something about you that reminds me of Tinkerbell in Peter Pan, she always made me feel good and happy and she was always flitting around."

He loved to travel and so did I, so soon we began to make arrangements to get married. He even got down on his knee for me. We laughed and cried, and it was beautiful. The date was set for December 14, 1985. We had lived together for one year.

CHAPTER 19

The Wedding

We decided to have the wedding at my family home in Northridge. The house was large and lovely and had a beautiful stairway in the front room and a huge back lawn for tables. The kitchen was very large for a cook to prepare the dinner and goodies for our big day.

I wore Mom's wedding dress with a few alterations. She had worn it loose in the style of the twenties, and I had it slightly taken in. It was so delicate and truly beautiful—made in France in the flapper style. I wondered how it kept so well after so many years. I was so proud to be wearing it, and it made her so happy. But I missed my dad.

I invited my closest friends and family, and Bill invited his, including some of his family from Northern California, like his sister Lillian and her husband, Saul.

There were about ninety people there. Nino walked me down the aisle—or, rather, down the stairs—to the nondenominational preacher. The stairway railing and the house was decorated in lilac and white flowers. Bill looked so handsome in his dark gray pinstriped suit, a gray silk tie, and lilac handkerchief in his lapel pocket.

Our wonderful pianist and great friend, Andy Thomas, played "All the Things You Are" during the ceremony, at Bill's request. Our family and friends all gathered around us; Mom and Nino were close by.

Instead of a long ceremony, we decided we would both write down our feelings and what we wanted to say to each other as we were married. All I can remember saying is, "What took you so long, my darling? I've been waiting for you all of my life." Everyone cried, including us. My cousin Carmen Donia said it was the most touching wedding she had ever been to, and as the principal of a high school, she had attended a lot of weddings!

We had many hors d'oeuvres served during the day, and I selected the dinner, which was lasagna with lots of cheeses and meatballs, a chicken and vegetable dish, hot garlic rolls, and two or three salads. Bill picked the huge wedding cake that he had made out of chocolate napoleons—his favorite.

Lennie Poncher took pictures all day with a new Panasonic video camera, and at the end of the day, he handed the whole camera over to us with the film intact. It was our wedding present. I guess since he introduced us to each other, it was apropos, but it was certainly unexpected!

For years, I have kept a copy of a phrase I once read: *Words to describe a happy marriage: "When love and skill work together, expect a miracle."* Bill and I try.

On our honeymoon, we went to Guadalajara, Mexico, for ten days. We traveled in our new beige casual safari-type pants and jackets. We even had safari hats and decided to wear them when we got off the plane so we wouldn't have to carry them. As we were walking to our luggage, I said, "How will the hotel driver we are supposed to meet ever recognize us?" Just at that very moment, we passed by some large full-length mirrors. Did we laugh! We decided we were very recognizable—even obvious! In fact, the driver came right up to us.

Being in Guadalajara was a perfect honeymoon. We saw all of the sights. The mariachis, of course, were everywhere and the best. Tlaquepaque was such an interesting area. We bought a brass stork that is almost four feet high and still have it in our home. It stands by the fireplace. We bought hanging parrots and pictures and jewelry and all the while the mariachis were still playing everywhere. It was a glorious honeymoon!

Soon we were home, and I was a married woman. You have no idea how strange that all felt. As you know, I had never been married before, and I was older than most women are when they take the step. So when Bill first introduced me to people as his wife, I thought how strange that sounded and felt. *I'm his wife?*

Bill had been married three times. First when he was just eighteen and in the maritime service to his high school sweetheart, Doris High. She was beautiful with big blue eyes, lovely features, and brownish hair which accounts for all of the beautiful women in his family. Their firstborn was Laura, who was pretty enough to be in the movies. Next was Bob, and then Gary. Two really handsome guys!

Bill's second wife was Nora Price, and she had a six-year-old boy named Michael, who Bill raised. Bill's daughter, Laura, has two lovely daughters named Erin and Bree. Bree has a daughter, Macee, which makes Bill and me great-grandparents. How can that be? Me, a great-grandmother?

Bill's son Bob has never married. When I met Gary and Bill that night at Angie's Restaurant, Gary was married to Suzanne, and they had one son, Justin, who was three years old. We had lunch with them soon after our honeymoon, and as we were all sitting down at the table, Suzanne said something I will never forget. To little Justin, she said, "Sit next to *Grandma* April." Needless to say, I couldn't believe it was me she was talking about. I just stared at her. Again, a shock, but I was getting used to them. Then Justin called me "Apple," and I laughed.

Grandma Apple! It was so strange to be called all of these names when I had been plain April for so many years.

Please don't misunderstand. I am the luckiest person on this great earth. Grandma, great-grandma, stepmom, mother-in-law, bonus mom, whatever—anything these adorable people want to call me, I am happy to answer to. And I got them all with no effort! I guess it's just that it all came to me at once, not gradually, like it usually happens. Anyway, that's what I get for waiting all of my life (so many years) for Bill Perman to show up.

Gary and Suzanne had two more beautiful sons, Garrett and Blake, and then, I'm sorry to say, they got a divorce. Gary then married a wonderful, lovely, caring gal, Julie Cavanaugh. We all grew to love her so much, and she takes good care of all of Gary's boys. Sixteen years ago, she and Gary had a beautiful daughter they named Nicole. She is a cutie pie who calls me Grandma April, and I love it.

Bill is from Northern California, and that is where I met his mom, Celia, another beauty, before she passed away. Bill resembles her. I met his family—sister, aunts, uncles, and cousins. His family on his mom's side was in the auto supply business and was very successful. Bill's father was born in England and had very little family here. He died early on, so I didn't get to meet him. Bill is Jewish, and his family life was very similar to mine. He had a large close knit family of uncles, aunts and cousins. All were very social and fun loving. I felt right at home with all of them. His Mother (his father had passed away) and sister were very warm and made me feel like I have been part of the family forever.

We decided to go on a cruise; it was my very first. Alaska was available, so we took it, and although it wasn't the most desirable place to cruise, in my estimation, I enjoyed it so much that in years to come, we went again. We bought black fur jackets and fur hats and even enjoyed the cold weather there. I loved cruising. You pack once, unpack once, and that's it. Everything is done for you. Every other day, you can get off the ship, walk or drive around the town, and come back, and dinner is ready. What a pleasure!

Speaking of dinner, while we were on the ship, Bill went fishing for salmon one day and brought back a huge wild king salmon. We had the chef on board fix it for our dinner that night, and I must tell you that never in our lives have we tasted anything like it. Practically from the ocean into our mouths. The best!

I gradually met all of Bill's many wonderful friends. Most of them lived in Southern or Northern California.

A year after Bill resumed working with Lennie Poncher, he and Gary bought out Lennie's Automotive Division and started their own business, along with Bob, called the Perman Group.

The office was in the Valley, so Bill and I moved to a lovely house in Chatsworth. The Perman Group prospered for a couple of years, and then they got an offer they couldn't refuse from David Rognlien, a successful friend in the same business. So they merged, and the company is now called RPS Marketing. R is for Rognlien, P is for Perman, and S is for Steve Salustri, a *paisano* of mine from Niagara Falls, New York.

However, the office was in downtown Los Angeles, and it took Bill forever going back and forth on the freeway. So after a year, Bill retired for the third time. Then he came up with a novelty item called Car Pets. They were little scented animals that you hang on your car's rearview mirror. Bill had connections in China, and they were interested in the item, so in 1989, we went to China. I couldn't believe I was really going. Never a dull moment! We grabbed our fur jackets and hats from Alaska, and we were off. The plane ride was long, but so what? We were on our way to China!

Our hotel was in Shanghai, and as soon as we got in our room, we looked out of our windows to see the city. There were hardly any cars. Everyone was riding a bike. Thousands of them—all over.

Their customs were so different from ours. The food was either absolutely delicious or too strange for us to eat. I didn't eat it, anyway. As you know, I will eat anything, but not if it moves!

I bought a very pretty back polyester and wool sweater with a yellow print on it for a dollar from a street merchant who had beautiful clothes. I wore it everywhere and still do.

We went to a restaurant one night with friends, and there was a man walking around the tables, entertaining everyone by showing how to make pasta from a lump of dough with his hands only. I saw him do it—amazing! Most of the men in our party arrived at the restaurant riding their bikes. What a strange custom.

The next day, we had an appointment to go to the manufacturers on an island right off of Shanghai. We were on a strange-looking boat and sat in a small dining area around a table. Bill and I were so cold, we were snuggled up to each other. I had to go to the ladies room, but when I saw it, I came right back and said, "Forget it." The toilet was just a stream of water in the corner of the room. It was spotless but so ancient looking.

When we arrived, we went directly to the factory, and as soon as we walked in, they handed us hot rubber water bottles and some hot tea to drink to keep warm. There was no heat in the building. Didn't anyone have heat? The workers were all women sitting at sewing machines, wearing tons of clothes and smiling at us.

Right off that room was a room for their babies. There were about twenty babies in a special area with two women taking care of them. No one seemed to mind the cold but Bill and I, and the deal was made fast. The Car Pets did well. Mission accomplished! We then spent a few days in the magical region of Hong Kong and did some shopping.

We returned to Los Angeles shortly after, and it was great to be driving in the car and to see Car Pets hanging in other cars. What great memories.

Bill is a very creative man. He had so many ventures in his lifetime before settling in the manufacturer's automotive rep business. When he was first married, he was a butcher, cook, and baker in the maritime service. (He has yet to tackle the candlesticks.) He was a jeweler and an insurance man. He built boats, was an operator of sport fishing charters, and was an entrepreneur many times. He can fix anything that breaks, which comes in handy. I can fix nothing but can break everything!

He wasn't joking when he said he wanted to travel. We covered Mexico and saw all of the exotic cities and ports of interest. Some of the places we went to were France, Italy, Hawaii, the Caribbean, Alaska twice, Spain, Canada, the Panama Canal, Austria, Turkey, Greece, Morocco, Germany, Costa Rica, Yugoslavia, Jamaica, China, Egypt, and, my favorite, Africa on a safari.

Bill naturally wanted to meet Cary Grant after hearing our stories, so Mom put some spaghetti together with her famous meatballs. The plan was to have the dinner at Howard Koch's home in Beverly Hills. He was a movie producer and the head of Paramount Pictures at that time. Howard and his wife had been friends of ours for years, and Cary had made many films for him.

So on that day, Bill and I were sitting in the Koch's TV room in their home in Beverly Hills, watching a Lakers game when Cary and his then-wife, Barbara, walked in. After saying their hellos at the door, Cary walked toward Bill and me, smiling. Bill had a flute of champagne on the table. He put his hand out to shake hands and knocked over his drink, and it smashed on the floor.

Cary didn't notice it at all. He just continued shaking Bill's hand and smiling. He kissed me and introduced Barbara. It was amazing. Poor Bill—nerves will get you every time. But with Cary, it was certainly understandable.

Bill and Cary talked together at dinner, and Bill was surprised to learn that Cary was in the movie business only for the economics. During dinner, Cary put his hand on Mom's hand and said, "Anna, I miss Sam here." It was the first time we had been together since Dad had passed away.

In 1998, we were living in the Valley. I was driving with the radio on when I heard the report that Glenn McCarthy had died. I waited. There were no tears at all, and there haven't been any since.

We decided that we would not lease the house in Cabo any longer and that we would remodel it and go there from time to time. It was fun fixing it up. We had the walls in the kitchen and our master suite torn down. We made the back deck much larger and had the whole inside of the house painted a pale peach color with white woodwork.

Many of the neighbors brought others to see it. It was so lovely. I even talked Mom into coming down and spending a week with us. She loved the house. It was always called "Casa Shalom" (Home of Peace). She especially liked the enlarged deck with such a close view of the famous arches with the ocean that represents Cabo San Lucas. We had such a good time, shopping and all, and I was so happy to have her there. I couldn't do enough for her.

A few years back, she got a terrible case of shingles. It was devastating. At that time, they knew very little about it, what it was, or how to curb the pain. She had always had such a high tolerance for pain, but this disease just changed everything. She complained even of a small sliver on her finger, and most of all, a burning tongue. All of her nerve endings were raw, so every little

The Wedding

thing was overwhelmingly painful. We took her to many doctors, and finally, after nothing working, one doctor suggested she try the antidepressant Elavil, and that at least gave her some relief at last.

In 1991, we sold our house in Chatsworth and moved to an apartment in Brentwood. I didn't mind the drive to see Mom, and I remember always crying while driving, knowing her time was getting short.

While we were living in Brentwood, the OJ murders happened about a mile away. It was a sad time while we lived there. We watched the whole episode of OJ on the TV for what seemed forever. In fact, the young man, Ron Goldman, who was killed with OJ's wife, Nicole, worked at a restaurant we used to patronize. He was a waiter and a really sweet guy.

One night, Angie Dickinson came to dinner, and I cooked! Mom didn't come because she didn't feel well enough. What did I cook? What else but spaghetti? I had met Angie years before when June Nelson brought her to our home in Los Angeles. June was married to David Nelson of the famous Nelson family on a television program called *Ozzie and Harriet* and was very close to Angie. June was coming to dinner and asked if Angie could come. When Bill's son, Gary, heard about Angie coming, he invited himself to dinner, too. So it was Bill, June, Nino, Angie, Gary, and me for a fun evening.

Bill went down to meet Angie in the parking garage of our condominium when she arrived. He was a great fan of hers, so I know he was nervous. But he managed quite well. Angie is a doll and loves to laugh, so Bill was in his glory. It was a delicious and comical evening.

Soon after, Mom began to feel ill. Again, we took her to many doctors, even in Beverly Hills, but there was no saving her. She had stomach cancer. Nino had been staying at the house with her, and we hired a woman to help. Mom had to have two major stomach operations. Toward the end, I, too, stayed at the house with her.

On her last night, my Aunt Elaine and Uncle Dom and Bill were there at the house. Nino and I were at Mom's bedside, and she said, "I want you both to know that I am so proud of you. Raising you has been my greatest joy. You didn't reach the heights in show business that you could have, but you did have some success, and I look at you now, and I still like what I see in your eyes, so maybe this is the best way." Then she said, "I don't know where I'm going from here, but if there is a place, it would be wonderful. If not, then it's a long sleep, and that's OK, too."

Nino and I were crying, and I heard him telling her that we would be all right and not to worry and for her to just let go whenever she wanted to. I couldn't take it and ran upstairs to my old bedroom and into the closet just to let out the scream that I felt was coming. They heard me downstairs, and Bill and Nino came running up to me. They couldn't understand how I screamed just at the moment Mom stopped breathing.

I don't have to tell you what life is like without her. Thank God for Bill. To this day, I hear Nino saying, "I don't know how I'm making it without her." She was eighty-six. It was June 29, 1992, when she left us.

I miss her every day. For years after she was gone, I got an urge to call her every single day. After all these years, I still get a faint reminder, as long as a heartbeat, that I must call her.

I take much joy in knowing that I am a part of my two wonderful parents. I carry them with me every day, no matter where I go, and there is no greater comfort.

In 1993, we were still in Brentwood and decided to move to Scottsdale, Arizona, in a brand-new development called the Ancala Country Club. Gary and his family had already moved to Scottsdale, and we wanted to be close to our growing grandchildren.

We visited Gary and found Scottsdale to be the cleanest city with the loveliest ambience. The freeways were beautifully manicured with not a sign of graffiti. And there were shopping areas like I had never seen! It's like being on vacation every day. The only downsides are the tremendously long, hot summers and missing Nino in Los Angeles.

We moved to Scottsdale into a brand-new, very lovely villa on a beautiful street in Ancala Country Club. Our backyard has a raised deck, and it overlooks the golf course with the most beautiful view of Camelback Mountain in the distance. The sunsets are gorgeous. Our neighbors are wonderful people. Unfortunately, most of them are "snowbirds," and they leave for their home states in the summer.

CHAPTER 20

Africa

In 1995, we met the Haywards, Louis and Dossie. They also lived in Ancala Country Club on our street during the winter months. They were about ten years older than we were, but they were raring to go anywhere and at any time. When they heard that we were planning a trip to Africa on a safari, they wanted to go in the worst way, and there was no stopping them. They were fun people, and we really grew to love them.

One day, Dossie said, "Now, April, you have to realize that I am quite a bit older than you, so you will have to consider that and slow down a bit." Well, it turned out to be just the opposite. She had more energy than I ever did! It shouldn't have surprised me as both of them were high-ranking officers in WWII. He was a major, and she was a captain in the medical corps and was even awarded a Bronze Star! So they were doers, and I have always been a "donter."

In 1997, we got our shots and were on our way to Africa. It was a dream of mine that I never ever thought would be fulfilled. Bill certainly brought adventure into my life along with love and children.

We left in February, and the plane trip was so much fun as we made friends in our group. It was a long haul, and our first stop was Nairobi, Kenya, to spend the night at the Elephant Walk Hotel. What an unusual place it was. As we walked into the foyer, there was a full-size stuffed elephant before us. It was monstrous in size, and it looked so real. Our room was also different looking because of the African ambience. The bed was a king size with a canapé mosquito net around it. Thank God! But I didn't see one bug while I was in Africa. The pictures and wall pieces were typical of where we were. They included animal pictures, beautiful carvings, and a great large map of Africa.

The next morning, our anticipation was mounting as before us was our tour of Nairobi. We flew an old DC-3 airplane to the Masai. It is a vast expanse of open plain with exotic trees as far as the eye can see. It is the home of all of nature's wild animals and the Masai tribe. Then, the Haywards, Bill, and I were assigned to our Rover and our driver, Anthony. The poor man was deluged with questions. I wish I could find the words to tell you how excited we were.

We drove along toward our camp, and after about half an hour, our eyes almost popped out! There, on the side of the road, very close to us, a pride of lions was feeding on an animal. We couldn't believe it. We saw a male and four or five baby lions. The female, a few feet away was sitting on her haunches waiting for them to finish so that she could pounce on the leftovers. What a sight. I don't know how to tell you the squeals that came from our Rover as we observed the scene. Our cameras and videos were going nonstop. And to think, we had just arrived!

The camp was a very large hut, so we checked in as though we were in a hotel. There were some small shops around it, and toward the back was the buffet-style dining room. It was very colorful. We had a delicious lunch. Practically anything you wanted was there, and it was all so tasty. There were all kinds of salads, rice, sandwiches, pastas, and meats; a sweet type of chicken with pineapple that was delicious and desserts I had never seen, including lots of custards and fruits.

Our accommodations were just what I was hoping for. They had a bit of the jungle flavor and were very clean. There were about thirty tents surrounding the large hut. They were about twenty feet wide and twenty five feet long. The tops were made of wood and the floors were tile, but they were definitely tents and zipped up at night. Each tent contained two twin beds, a closet, two dressers, and two chairs. The bathrooms were tiled, and the whole tent was very nicely done and was very comfortable and clean.

There was a tall fence around the whole compound to keep the animals out. Guards walked along the walkways at night, and we could hear the chimpanzees and other animals while we slept. If the chimpanzees flying through trees happened to get too close to us in our tents, the guards would push them away with long sticks.

Were we really in Africa? The knowledge that we would be there for seven whole days was mind-boggling!

The next morning, we were up at six o'clock. We met the Haywards for breakfast; their tent was just across from ours. We took off in our Rover for our African adventures.

While we were there, we saw herds of elephants, giraffes, beautiful zebras, a cheetah asleep under a tree, hyenas, all kinds of wild and gorgeous birds, and wild dogs that were mean and ugly looking. We watched hundreds of beautiful animals of different species running from predators and others feeding on vegetation or drinking from streams. We were in the Serengeti Plains in the Masai Mara. The tribes of people who live there are called Masai.

At one time, we were surrounded by a family of elephants that threatened to turn us over. We stayed absolutely still until they moved on. Exciting but frightening.

After the third day, I was tired and just wanted to take it easy, so we did. But Dossie wanted to continue to see the animals, and they did. What energy they had!

On the night before we went to visit one of the villages of the Masai tribe, I was told that when a really sick person in the tribe is dying, they pick that person up and put him or her in the bushes for the animals. That had quite an effect on me; I was freaked out. I got really frightened at the very thought of that. I spoke to Bill, and he said that Anthony, our driver, told us that story and that it was true. However, I learned that the person they put out for the animals was already dead. I was concerned because I felt it was an awfully unbearable way to treat your dead loved ones. I know I was in Africa and that traditions were different, but it was such a scary feeling.

On that night, during our dinner, we were told that after dinner we would be entertained by fifteen of the Masai warriors. We could hear them coming from the beat of the drums and the chanting that came from off in the distance.

They arrived in their colorful African wraps. They were extremely tall young men with huge, heavy sticks and beautifully carved clubs that they carried at their sides. They were very imposing looking. They sang and danced wildly and jumped into the air. It looked like they were trying to see who could jump the highest. Then they began grunting, and the sound was so guttural and primitive that it kind of frightened me again.

The next morning we were up at six o'clock. It was so cold that I put on a long-sleeved, tight wool sweater. However, by the time we arrived at the Masai village around ten-thirty, we were sweltering. The temperature was close to 106 degrees and rising.

After traveling about thirty minutes, we went into the brush-fenced circle where all of the huts were. There were about fifteen huts made of cow dung, and the smell was unforgiving, especially in the sun. We all took pictures and bought some beads that the women made, and all the while it was getting hotter and hotter. I wondered how all of them—men, women, and children—fit into those tiny huts. I peeked into one, and it was only about ten feet wide and fifteen feet long and had a mesquite fire pit in the center of the dirt floor. Forget about air-conditioning.

Bill tried to talk to a man who was sitting on the ground up against his hut. The man and his children were sitting by the hut in the direct heat without any shade, staring at me. All of his wives were there, too. I was really sweating in that wool sweater, and with all of the humidity, my hair had frizzed up, so I was not a pretty sight.

Bill said that he liked the man's carved club, and he asked him if he could buy it. He offered him money, but the man refused. When Bill asked if there was anything he could trade for the club, the man pointed at *me*. Needless to say, I was very nervous.

I don't know what was wrong with me; I usually take things so lightly. I laughed it off, but my heart wasn't in it. However, Bill did buy the club. He doesn't remember what he paid for it, but I know it wasn't me! I was OK when we returned to the camp. I guess the story about the Masai tribe putting their dead in the bushes for the animals just got to me.

The trip was unforgettable. I'll never forget the feelings, especially the joy. Also, I will always remember the beautiful, unbelievable scenery of colors and greenery and flowers and trees that I had never imagined before. Some of the plants and flowers were gigantic, the scents were heavenly, and the spectacular African Acacia trees standing in the savannah in the Masai Mara were like none we had ever seen. They were remote looking and anything but symmetrical. And, because they were usually standing by themselves, they looked rather lonely.

We went to Egypt after our safari, and it was also a dream come true for me. I saw the pyramids, the Sphinx, many temples, and all of the burial spots. Like the people of Africa, the

Egyptian people could not have been more gracious. Smiles greeted us everywhere we went.

We took a ride on the Nile River on a traditional Egyptian boat called a felucca. Being a sailor, Bill eventually talked the captain in letting him take command, and he sailed us to our destination. It was a beautiful adventure.

We visited the camel rides near the pyramids, and the men talked Dossie into getting on one. She immediately yelled, "Come on, April!" Everyone's eyes were on me. As soon as I reluctantly got on, the camel stretched its long neck downward, and I felt myself sliding down. Bill got on with me, pulled me up, and we both held on for dear life—and for pictures. Then, we tried to get off. That was a joke. We both almost fell off! We have a video of it, and it is hilarious. My final words on the video as I got off were "Forget it!" Louis and Dossie were still on the camel, smiling and waving, as we walked away. They were unbelievable.

Then we all took a horse and buggy ride to one of the many tourist stores, where all four of us bought the customary long cotton robes everyone wore in Egypt called galipeas.

Bill tried his royal blue one on, with a white turban on his head, and one of the men in our group said, "Bill, I'll bet you twenty dollars you won't wear that whole outfit to dinner tonight at the hotel." When six-thirty came around, Bill walked into the dining room in his blue galipea and white turban and picked up twenty bucks and lots of laughs.

The vacation was fabulous. Thanks to Abercrombie and Fitch Tour Agency—and my husband for taking me there and on so many adventures.

CHAPTER 21

Pinetop

In 1998, the summer heat here in Scottsdale was really getting to us. I think it was around 116 degrees, and it doesn't cool off at night. It was unbearable, so we drove up to Pinetop during the summer months to get some relief. It was three hours by car and twenty degrees cooler. Most of our friends in Ancala went back to their home states around May because of our long, terribly hot summers. They returned around October or November.

We bought a lovely condo on the golf course in Pinetop, and Bill, who had also played in Scottsdale, got heavily into the game. I tried to play and even got some golf clubs, but it wasn't really important to me, and it hurt my back—although I do love watching it on television.

Pinetop is located in the largest Ponderosa pine forest in the country. Pine trees were everywhere, and there wasn't a cactus in sight. I prefer the desert, but it was definitely cooler—twenty degrees cooler.

We drove back and forth to Scottsdale about every three or four weeks to check on the house and for doctor appointments. We did that from June to the latter part of September.

In 1999, we sold Casa Shalom in Cabo San Lucas, Mexico, and in 2002, we sold the condo in Pinetop and bought a three-bedroom house there. The house was very charming and about a year old. We fixed things and added to the kitchen. The layout was lovely, and every room seemed to flow into the next.

We were there for about ten years. I cooked a lot, and when Bill wasn't playing golf, he cooked. I bought furniture at the local shops and went to lots of garage sales, art shows, and flea markets. We made wonderful friends, and I read a lot of wonderful books.

Then, in 2010, we decided the altitude (seventy-five hundred feet) was too high for us, so we sold the house. Now we are back in the heat of the summer until we can think of somewhere to go next.

CHAPTER 22

Buffalo Music Hall of Fame

Oh, I must tell you. In 1999, Nino and I got word that we were being inducted in the Buffalo Music Hall of Fame. We were invited to go there for the occasion. Needless to say, Nino and I were thrilled, but he was unable to go. Bill and I went to Niagara Falls and stayed with my Aunt Elaine and Uncle Dom Mancini. Buffalo is only fourteen miles from Niagara.

It was quite an event, and they even sent a limousine to pick us up. Bill, me, and two of my aunts, Sarah and Isabel, in a limo made a very funny scene. We all had some drinks and got silly on the way home. It made me realize how much I miss them all.

At the ceremony, I got up and gave a short thank-you speech. They presented me with two small statuettes with our names on them with a silver buffalo on top. How thoughtful of them, and how appreciative we were.

Niagara Falls is home. Although I lived in Los Angeles many more years than I did Niagara, it is still home. I left there when I was twelve years old, but I was born there and still have my family there, so it will always be home. When I now visit there, as I approach Pine Avenue, there is a huge sign that says "Little Italy." How right they are.

I have three aunts left who are getting on in years. The youngest, Elaine, is the closest to me, so she is more like a sister. I never called her *Aunt* Elaine. She was always just Elaine. She helped me with everything during my career and even traveled with me for a while. I miss her very much, but I go to see them all about every two years back in Niagara Falls.

One of my aunts, Sarah, is 104 years old, and Isabel, the seamstress, is ninety-nine. Also, I have many cousins on my Mom's side and a few on my Dad's, so Niagara Falls is always a fun trip. However, when I get ready to leave there for Arizona, I get a little frightened because of everyone's age; they may not be there when I return. It's a difficult and sad thought. On summer nights, we could hear the roar of the Falls since we lived just a few miles away. Although I lived there for twelve years, I hardly ever saw the Falls. I had to wait until I was married, when Bill took me to see the Maid of the Mist and the different spectacular views of the Falls on both the United States and Canadian sides. What an unforgettable sight.

It's strange, but it seems that if people live in a place where there is a popular attraction, they hardly ever get to see it. The city of Niagara could have profited greatly with the beauty of its surroundings, but for some reason or another, it never did.

CHAPTER 23

The Present

I now have nine grandchildren and two great-grandchildren. Justin, Gary's oldest son—the one who at three years old called me Grandma Apple—is now married. He and his lovely wife, Melissa, had an adorable baby girl a year ago called Haley Jane. Another baby is on its way. (a little boy, Aidan)

I love my life with Bill. He has been more than I ever could have imagined, and he has shared all of his beautiful children with me. Life is good.

We are still living at Ancala Country Club in Scottsdale, Arizona. I go to see Nino or he comes here every three or four months. Missing Nino and not having him close by is the only unhappiness I feel, but we are thinking of moving closer to Los Angeles.

I miss singing, but I guess I always will. I wish I had done more to entertain you, but I am so happy you enjoyed what I did. I love hearing from you and will always try to answer.

I can't believe I have finished this book. However, I wrote it for you, and I guess if you are supposed to read it, you will. Otherwise, my grandchildren will learn many interesting things about their grandmother.

Take good care, my dear friends, and know that singing for you has been one of my greatest thrills.

With love,

April

Please visit me at www.teachmetiger.net and e mail me at april@teachmetiger.net

Epilogue

As I said, I was born on April 29, 1929, in Niagara Falls, New York. I do want you to know how very difficult it is for me to write my birthdate down on paper. I have always assumed that if I ever wrote my life story, I would have to tell the truth about my age. That's why it took me so long. I couldn't hide it any longer.

I have, for most of my life, because when Glenn McCarthy and I were over, I was almost thirty years old. Then I was in the rock and roll era, singing with Nino. At that time, most of the singers were in their late teens or early twenties. Nino was twenty-four. When people would ask who was older, we said (after we talked it over), that Nino was a couple of years older. That sounded good, and Nino didn't mind. I don't feel my age. I still can't write the number down for you. You will have to figure it out.

I have been so blessed with good health, and I thank God every day of my life for all that he has given me. I hope I don't look my age, but who knows? Anyway, so far-so good.

Mom's Recipes

I am a food hound. I really am. I love, love, love to eat. I could easily be very fat, but at an early age, I decided I would not be a fat singer. I would taste food and be somewhat satisfied. For instance, after dinner, instead of dessert, I would have a teaspoon of jam; for lunch, I had half a sandwich; and instead of a full dish of spaghetti, I would have just a half. Well, I must admit it is tough to eat half of a dish of spaghetti. I usually cheat on that. I still eat that way today, and it's a way of life.

My grandparents had a restaurant, but that had nothing to do with my desire for food. I was born hungry, as my mom used to say. I went to see my grandparents every day. They lived only two blocks from our apartment on Pine Avenue. They were always at the restaurant, he at the bar, she in the kitchen.

I would go to the house behind the restaurant, where my pretty, sexy aunts, my mother's younger sisters, lived. They were so much fun and wore such pretty clothes. I was closest to Elaine, the youngest. I loved trying on her shoes. She always knew I had been into the boxes because the shoes were always in backward. I do a lot of things backward.

My nonna's cooking specialty was spaghetti sauce with meatballs. She also cooked an Italian steak under the broiler with garlic and oregano. Delicious! It was my grandfather's favorite. Also, after her chicken soup was cooked, using the same hamburger mixture as her larger meatballs with the spaghetti sauce, she rolled up little meatballs, a little larger than the size of a marble, and dropped them in hot soup. They would cook immediately. Then she would add a bit of cooked orzo. It was so good. Today, I think you can buy the soup in a can. It's called Sicilian Wedding Soup, but it doesn't taste as good as hers or my mom's.

When I was young, our playground was on Fifteenth and Pine Avenue. My grandparents' restaurant, the Rainbow Grill, and my dad's grocery store were on the corner. My grandfather's apartment building was there, as were my cousins and all of my playmates and lots of food. What more could I ask for? The Rainbow movie theater was right across the street, and it had the best popcorn. What a life.

When we went to Los Angeles, Mom cooked spaghetti and meatballs for all of our friends. I served and helped with the dishes. Cary Grant, Liberace, all of our many managers, the producer Howard Koch, Ahmet Ertegun, the Righteous Brothers, Phil Spector and Angie Dickinson, Ozzie and Harriet, and David Nelson were among the many that came to eat.

David put ketchup on Mom's spaghetti sauce; she almost fainted. David married June Blair, who used to be Nino's girlfriend. She was a beautiful redhead and became very close to our family. When she married David, we were still friends, and we went to the wedding and all became like family.

Mom's Spaghetti Sauce and Meatballs

Serves four
1 ½ lb. meat (pork and beef or chicken)
¼ to ½ onion minced
4 to 5 cloves garlic, minced
Three 14 ½ oz. cans of peeled or crushed tomatoes (Hunt's is best)
One or two 14 ½ oz. cans of tomato sauce
One 6 oz. can of tomato paste (Contadina with Italian herbs)
½ tsp. sugar (or more to taste)
½ tsp. black pepper
½ tsp. fennel seed
1 tsp. fresh basil and some pesto (as much as you like)
1 tbsp. salt
Pinch baking soda

First, brown meat, drain excess oil, and place meat in dish. In same pan, cook minced onion and garlic until golden brown. Return meat to pan, and add crushed tomatoes, or if using whole peeled tomatoes, squash as you put in pan with browned meat and cooked onions and garlic.

Next, add tomato paste and water (two cans water per can of paste) and the tomato sauce. Add next four ingredients and after a half hour of cooking on medium, add salt and baking soda.

Continue cooking meat on medium heat in sauce until tender (about one hour).

If sauce is too thick, add water. Season to taste again. Stir with wooden spoon often. Sauce is ready when meat is done.

Mom's Meatballs

(in her own words)

Serves four
1 lb. chuck meat or round steak—have butcher grind it for you
2 eggs
½ cup Italian-style bread crumbs
¼ cup Roman or Parmesan or any other grated cheese
1 tsp. salt
¼ tsp. pepper
½ tsp. fresh parsley or basil

Combine all with half cup of water or more to make meatballs firm but soft enough to fry. Fry golden brown in olive oil. When one side is brown, turn the meatball over. When they are cooked, add to spaghetti sauce. Good luck.

Do not handle the meatball mixture more than you have to. When you are about to fry the meatballs in oil, wet your hands and get enough of the meatball mixture for the meatball. Then pat it just enough to hold it together. It doesn't have to be perfectly round.

You can also bake them. Enjoy.

Letters from Servicemen

---Original Message---
Subject: Wonderful April Memories
Date: Thu, 25 Apr 2013 11:11:22-0700

Happy Birthday, Ms Stevens,

In the summer of 1967, a new class of plebes—the Class of 1971—entered the United States Naval Academy at Annapolis, Maryland. From big cities, small cities, suburbs, and rural towns and hamlets across America, and some foreign countries, they had come. Back in those days, America's service academies were all-male bastions, uncorrupted by the kind of tolerant, multiculturally-divrerse, politically-correct, coed, sexual harassment baloney defining the service academies today. For incoming classes, the two months of Plebe Summer were hours, stretching into days, of bewilderment, terror, torture, loneliness, M-1 thumbs, public humiliation, and raging testosterone.

Midshipmen from the Class of 1969—hand-selected by the institution for their qualities of meanness and their ability to holler at the tops of their lungs for no reasnos readily apparent—provided the instruction and discipline necessary to mold these fine young men into the kind of trained and motivated steely-eyed killers that would be suitable for integration into the Brigade of Midshipmen. After taps (lights out), as part of their master plan to break us in body, mind and spirit, these ham-handed, knuckle-dragging, brutish, no-neck martinets of '69 would play recordings of you, Ms Stevens, softly purring to us over the general announcing system in Bancroft Hall. The idea was to make us yearn for podunks and for girlfriends left behind…."who-wuh-wuh-who-WOH!"

I suppose that it worked on a few of the "weak sisters," but for the rest of us, you came to symbolzie all of the things for which American fighting men once proudly fought and died. Listening to you only made us stronger. You gave us the resolve that we needed to improvise, adapt, and overcome; to prepare ourselves morally, mentally, and physically to fight to the death the communist menace, just to keep Mom and Sis—and you, yourself, Ms Stevens—from the reeducation camps and the gulags.

I returned from a recent "mini-reunion" of a handful of us "Men of USNA '71 (12th Company)." One participant brought a tape recording of you singing "Teach Me Tiger" that he had recorded from the radio. Although we now are gray and in varying states of creakiness and decay, I will testify that you still are well and warmly remembered by all of us. You should have seen the way that you rekindled the fire in our eyes as we reminisced among ourselves, with you urging us on in the background.... "who-wuh-wuh-who-WOH!"

Someone asked whether any of us ever had written to you to thank you, and to tell you what you had meant to us in those days and even now. I said that I would see whether you have a personal page on facebook. Not finding one, I decided to try forwarding this sentimental reminscence to the address given for the editor of the Nino and April website, for forwarding on to you. We so want you to know, on the anniversary of your birth, the story of our unrequited love for a sexy, sensual, timeless, and truly beautiful lady.

With greatest love, appreciation, and thanks, from the Men of USNA '71 (12th Company). No matter how many birthdays you celebrate, you are forever young and beautiful in our collective memory and in our hearts.

Your unworthy champion,
James Yeakley, USNA '71 (12th Company)

Herschel Hughes, Jr.
CDR, MSC, USNR (Ret.)
October 26, 2006

April Stevens Perman

Dear April,

   I want to thank you personally, and especially for my 12th company mantes, and for my classmates as a whole, for your kind participation in our U.S. Naval Academy Class of 1966 40th reunion.

   The CD's Mr. Chaffins ent, and the pictures and note you sent, were a TREMENDOUS, I repeat TREMENDOUS, success at our reunion. All of the men of 12th company were ecstatic about their pictures and the sentiment of your n ote. They were presented at our company dinner held Thursday, September 21, at the Lord Calvert Hotel, one of the historic inns of Annapolise located across the street from the state capitol, the symbol you see on the "Maryland" quarters.

   Following our meal, each of us took turns bringing each other up to date on our lives. At the close of my personal comments about my wife, family, and myself, I remarked that I had a gift for each of them—"something very special." Then, with the deepest and warmest smile I have felt in years, I told them what you ahd done for us and read your note to them. Following that, I handed out the pictures you provided. They were on their feet with excitement and lavished praise on us both as they opened the envelopes with incredulity. One even asked me, "Is this for real? You're not putting one over on us are you?" But I reminded them ever so gently that these gifts were due to your graciousness and that the person behind the "young men's fantasies" that we had all enjoyed in our youth was, indeed, a very special lady. I then played "Teach Me Tiger" from the CD provided by Mr. Chaffin and reminded them that this "performance" really was just for them!

After our personal remarks, we began the traditional round of toasts with some of the best port wine I have ever tasted. I want you to know that you were formally toasted by 12th Company, U.S. Naval Academy Class of 1966, during that round of toasts that included the Commander-in-Chief, the Commandment of the Marine Corps, the Chief of Naval Operations, our dear wives, and many more well respected and loved persons, ships, and naval victories.

Also, I am happy to report that the Superintendent of the U.S. Naval Academy, Rod Rempt, also a classmate, spontaneously mentioned you in his formal welcome to our whole class during a brief about current academy developments. Also, at the class wide formal dinner dance on Saturday night following Navy's football game, our class president, Mike Haskins, passed on your best wishes, as expressed in your note, to the entire class, and, of course, we played "Teach Me Tiger" one time.

Thank you, again, so much, for your paticipation in our reunion from all the men of 12th company, and I think I can confidently speak for the entire class, as well, on this issue. And, apparently, even for some of the wives, too! With Warm Regards,

Jon H. Barton, Sr.

April 15, 2007

Dear April,

At this very late date, please accept my profound gratitude for your beautiful music and your photo and letter to commemorate our USNA '66 40th reunion. I hope this finds you well and happy. I am so proud of Herschel for getting in touch with you and so appreciative of *Teach Me, Tiger*, a true gift to us all. It is ironic that you thanked us for including our memories of you in our reunion. Actually, it is **we** who should thank **You**.

I had intended to write you long before now, and was reminded during the process of doing income tax the last few days: I have a computer desktop icon so that I can play *Teach Me, Tiger* with two mouse clicks, and I must have listened to you 50 or more times during taxes, which eased the pain a lot. I like to hear it repeat about twice, so obviously the original should have been about six minutes long, instead of 2:22! (I purchased the song from Walmart.com, and it is absolutely the best 88 cents I have spent in my life.)

Your comment about waking up the *Challenger* crew prompted me to search NASA to see if either of our two Classes of '66 astronauts was behind it. In the process, I discovered the Nino and April website, which is great. Your brother, as one would expect, is a very nice-looking man, and I loved reading about your adventures and successes. Please relay to Nino my regards and congratulations.

Enclosed is the composite photo that wife Jan and I included in our Christmas cards. As you can see, I am really into grandfather-hood after my 37-year (Navy and Delta) flying career. Those precious children know *Anchors Aweigh*. When they get older, the boys will know *Teach me, Tiger*.

I don't think Herschel would mind my sharing that he told me about having your photo and letters framed (Anne calls it his 'shrine'). I think I'll do the same thing, and include some of the website photos.

April, one of my prayers is that I leave the world better in some ways than it was when I entered it. You have, through your music, made the world a better place for so many of us.

Thank you, again, Sweet Lady, and may God Bless You,

Jon

Peter Schittler

Dear Ms. Stevens,

It's finally time to **thank you** for your music and the entertainment these have given us (and continue to do so), a couple of music lovers, through the years!

You have given the world a series of unforgettable gems, some of which have accompanied me 11 my life. "Deep Purple" or the sultry "Teach me Tiger" never ever really left my emmory after I heard them first (and it looks like they never will), but I don't want to bore you with a list you know yourself better! I sincerely hope you are as proud to have recorded these great songs as we are listening to them!

I enclose two photo montages I made myself and politely ask if you could sign one to PETER, and one to FARHAT (a buddy of mine and fan as well whom I'd like to surprise with an autographed picture). Also, there is a third one enclosed justin case you'd like to keep one for yourself!

There are € 8.—which would be OK for return postage.

Finally, in case you've never been here, I enclose a picture postcard from beautiful Vienna!

Thank you very much!

Sincerely,

Peter

---Original Message---
Subject: To Mrs. Stevens
Date: Thu, 28 Feb 2013 19:10:53-0800
From: Hans Liebscher

Dear Mrs. Stevens,

Growing up in Germany, your "Teach me Tiger" was one of the most fascinating songs of my boyhood.
I was looking to get this song for decades, now with the Internet and YouTube it is all so easy.
This song is one of the most beautiful songs ever. Sexy and "innocent" at the same time, most credits belong to your absolute fantastic voice.
I am still fascinated by this song as when I haerd it for the first time. I could listen to your song for hours, you were one of one of the reasons for me to learn English so I could understand what this beautiful voice had to say.
Living for almost 30 years in Southern California I made it here to the top of my trade and I have a assignment coming up in Palm Springs. It involves restoration and copper smiting work at the former Harlow Residence in Palm Springs.
You would make me the luckiest Man if I could invite you and your husband for dinner at a place of your choice in the Palm Springs area.

Best wishes,

Hans Liebscher

April Stevens

When we hear your soft sensual tones floating through our room, we feel ourselves carried away to a world of love and ecstasy. All our troubles are erased and we find ourselves reposing on the proverbial pink cloud. To us, you are the epitome of feminine charm."

"On my disk-jockey program, The Voice of The Desert, in Saudi Arabia, you are one of my favorite recording artists, and as for the rest of the base, more of your records are requested than any other artist. Please keep them coming, you are doing the morale of this isolated base wonders… *Dharan, Saudi Arabia*"

"Darling, your voice! You don't know how much your songs mean to my men. Something like you is what all of us is fighting for. They all wanted me to write for them. We want your photograph immediately. So darling, don't let us down, we aren't (letting) you (down). We are trying our best over here. So please don't let us down…" M/Sgt Front Lines, Korea

"You have a voice that's two parts heaven and one part hell. It makes you feel like bending an iron bar. You feel like cussing and crying and writing a letter to your girl and putting a lot of mush in it, that you never knew you knew…"

"Every time someone who has heard 'Don't Do It' is asked to describe it, he is seized by what amounts to convulsions and an expressino that closely approximate that of a starved dog dreaming of a T-bone steak. You have quite an effect on a man under normal conditions, imagine what it is like when you haven't seen a woman for ten months…" Aleutians

Discography
Single Releases

1950
"No, No, No, Not That"—Laurel SLS 7000-8000
"Black Lace"—Laurel SLS 7000-8000
"Voodoo"—Society 6-A
"Don't Do It"—Society 9-A
"The Sweetest Day"—Society 10-A
"Subway Express I—April with Robert Bice"—Society 11-A
"Subway Express II—April With Robert Bice"—Society 11-B
"Night in a Toy Shop Parts 1 and 2"—Society 12-A & B
"The Envelope and the Rope"—Society 13-A
"Shadow Waltz"—Society 13-B
"Later Perhaps (Not Now)"—Society 15-A
"End of Desire"—Society 15-B

1951
"My Lost Melody"—RCA Victor 4101B (Side A Instrumental "You Are The One")
"I'm in Love Again"—RCA Victor 4148
"Gimme a Little Kiss, Will Ya, Huh?"—RCA Victor 4208

"Dreamy Melody"—RCA Victor 4208
"And So To Sleep Again"—RCA Victor 4283
"Ah, C'mon"—RCA Victor 4283
"The Tricks of Trade"—RCA Victor 4381
"Put Me in Your Pocket"—RCA Victor 4381

1952
"I Love the Way You're Breaking My Heart"—RCA Victor 4567
"Meant to Tell You"—RCA Victor 4567
"That Naughty Waltz"—RCA Victor 4676
"I Like to Talk to Myself"—RCA Victor 4676

1953
"Hot Tamale"—King K1271
"Treat Me Nice"—King K1271
"How Could Red Riding Hood (Have Been So Very Good)"—King K1287
"You Said You'd Do It (Are You Gonna)"—King K1287
"C'est Si Bon"—King K6327
"Soft Warm Lips"—King K6330

1959
"Teach Me Tiger"—Imperial 5626
"That Warm Afternoon"—Imperial 5626

1960
"Fly Me to the Moon (In Other Words)"—Imperial 5666 & 5907
"Jonny"—Imperial 5666
"Ooeah (That's What You Do To Me)"—Nino & April—United Artists 261
"High School Sweetheart"—Nino & April—United Artists 261

1961
"Love Kitten"—Imperial 5761
"You and Only You"—Imperial 5761/Niagara 1635 (1976)/Chelsea 3052 (1976)

1962
"Big John"—April & Nino (as Carol & Anthony)—Capitol 4517
"Letter From a Train"—April & Nino (as Carol & Anthony)—Capitol 4517
"Sweet and Lovely"—April & Nino—Atco 6224
"True Love"—April & Nino—Atco 6224
"Paradise"—April & Nino—Atco 6248
"Indian Love Call"—April & Nino—Atco 6248

1963
"Baby Weemus"—April & Nino—Atco 6263
"(We'll Always Be) Together"—April & Nino—Atco 6263
"Deep Purple"—Nino & April—Atco 6273
"I've Been Carrying a Torch For You So Long That I Burned a Great Big Hole In My Heart"—Nino & April—Atco 6273
"Illusione" ("Deep Purple" in Italian)—Nino & April—Atlantic 90133X45 (Italy)

1964
"Whispering"—Nino & April—Atco 6281
"Tweedlee Dee"—Nino & April—Atco 6281
"Stardust"—Nino & April—Atco 6286
"1-45"—Nino & April—Atco 6286
"Tea For Two"—Nino & April—Atco 6294
"I'm Confessin' (That I Love You)"—Nino & April—Atco 6294
"Who"—Nino & April—Atco 6306
"I Surrender Dear"—Nino & April—Atco 6306
"Honeysuckle Rose" (Mono)—Nino & April—Atco 6325

"Our Love"—Nino & April—Atco 6325
"Memories of You"—Nino & April—Unreleased Atco Side
"More Than You Know"—Nino & April—Unreleased Atco Side
"Angelito"—Nino & April—Unreleased Atco Side
"Melancholy Baby"—Nino & April—Atco 6314
"Ooh La La"—Nino & April—Atco 6314
"Sabor a Mi"—Unreleased Atco Side

1965
"The Coldest Night of the Year"—Nino & April—Atco 6337
"These Arms of Mine"—Nino & April—Atco 6337
"Teach Me Tiger" 1965—Atco 6346
"Morning 'Til Midnight"—Atco 6346
"Swing Me"—Nino & April—Atco 6350
"Tomorrow Is Soon a Memory"—Nino & April—Atco 6350/Atco 6897 (1972)
"Think of You"—Nino & April—Atco 6360
"I'm Sweet on You"—Nino & April—Atco 6360
"I Love How You Love Me"—Nino & April—Atco 6375
"Tears of Sorrow"—Nino & April—Atco 6375

1966
"No Hair Sam"—Atco 6380
"Lovin' Valentine"—Atco 6380
"America's Weather Girl" (Spoken Word Radio Spots)—Atco Unknown Catalog "Number"—(Radio Station Release Only)
"Hey Baby"—Nino & April—Atco 6391
"Poison of Your Kiss"—Nino & April—Atco 6391
"Bye Bye Blues"—Nino & April—Atco 6410
"All Strung Out"—Nino & April—White Whale 236
"I Can't Go On Living Baby Without You"—Nino & April—White Whale 236/White Whale 252
"Little Child"—Nino & April—White Whale 252

Discography Single Releases

"Wings of Love"—Nino & April—White Whale 246/White Whale 268 (1968)/White Whale 271 (1968)

1967
"The Habit of Lovin' You Baby"—Nino & April—White Whale 241
"You'll Be Needing Me Baby"—Nino & April—White Whale 241
"My Old Flame"—Nino & April—White Whale 246 **
"Falling In Love Again"—MGM K13825
"Wanting You"—MGM K13825
"Feelin' Kinda Sunday"—Nino & April—MGM Unreleased Side

1968
"Let It Be Me"—Nino & April—White Whale 268
"Ooh Poo Pah Doo"—Nino & April—White Whale 271
"Please Help Me I'm Falling"—Nino & April—White Whale Unreleased Side
"Yesterday I Heard the Rain (Esta Tarde Vi Llover)"—Nino & April—Bell 769
"Did I or Didn't I"—Nino & April—Bell 769

1969
"Sea of Love/Dock of the Bay"—Nino & April—Bell 823
"Twilight Time"—Nino & April—Bell 823

1970
"Don't Think Twice, It's All Right"—Nino & April—Daddy Sam 1300

1971
"How About Me (It's Over)"—Nino & April—MGM 14266
"Making Love to Rainbow Colors"—Nino & April—MGM 14266
"I'd Start All Over with You Again"—Nino & April—MGM Unreleased Side
"Story of Love" (April Narration)—April—Verve 10661
"Story of Love" (Vocal Duet)—Nino & April—Verve Unreleased Side

1972
"Darling You Were All That I Had"—Nino & April—Marina 507
"You're Losing Me"—Nino & April—Marina 507
"She's My Baby"—Nino & April—Atco 6897
"Love Story"—Nino & April—A&M 1394
"Hoochy Coochy Wing Dang Doo"—Nino & April—A&M 1394

1973
"Put It Where You Want It"—Nino & April—A&M 1443
"I Can't Get Over You Baby"—Nino & April—A&M 1443

1974
"Wake Up and Love Me"—A&M 1528
"Gotta Leave You Baby"—A&M 1528/
"Who Turns Me On"—Nino & April—A&M SP 8255 (Europe Only)
"(Won't You) Marry Me Again"—A&M 1636
"Gotta Leave You Baby" (With Strings)—A&M 1636

1975
"You Turn Me On"—Nino & April—A&M 1674
"Never Had a Lover"—Nino & April—A&M 1674

1976
"What Kind of Fool Am I"—Nino & April—Niagara 1635/Chelsea 3052
"I Found My Man"—Unreleased Demo

1980
"Our Love"—Nino & April—Unreleased Horn Track
"I Wonder Who's Kissing Her Now"—Nino & April—Horn 3
"I Never Loved Anyone Like I Love You"—Nino & April—Horn 3

1983
"Would I Love You (Love You, Love You)"—Nino & April—unreleased track from film *Kiss My Grits*

1985
"Once Upon a Very Special Time—Palace PRS 500
"Lovers and Other Strangers—Palace PRS 500
"I'm Fallin' For You—Nino & April—Unreleased Demo

1999
"Why Do I Love You/Always"—April narration, Nino saxophone—unreleased demo

Vinyl Albums

<u>1960</u>
***Teach Me Tiger*—Imperial 12055**

Track Listing:
"Do It Again"
"Teach Me Tiger"
"I Want a Lip"
"Fly Me to the Moon (In Other Words)"
"I Get Ideas"
"Talk To Me"
"I'm in Love Again" (Re-Recorded)
"That's My Name"
"I'm Making Believe"
"I'll Wait For Your Love"
"It Can't Be Wrong"
"When My Baby Smiles At Me"

<u>1963</u>
***Deep Purple* (With Nino Tempo)—Atco 33-156 (Mono) and Atco SD 33-156 (Stereo)**

Track Listing:
"Deep Purple"
"Paradise"
"Baby Weemus"
"True Love"
"It's Pretty Funny"

"Tears of Sorrow"
"Sweet and Lovely"
"One Dozen Roses"
"(We'll Always Be) Together"
"Indian Love Call"
"Shine On Harvest Moon"
"I've Been Carrying a Torch for You So Long That I Burned a Great Big Hole in My Heart"

1964
Nino and April Sing the Great Songs **(With Nino Tempo)— Atco 33-162 (Mono) and Atco SD 33-162 (Stereo)**

Track Listing:
"Tea for Two"
"I'm Confessin' That I Love You"
"Honeysuckle Rose"
"Stardust"
"All the Things You Are"
"St. Louis Blues"
"Whispering"
"Begin the Beguine"
"My Blue Heaven"
"Who"
"I Surrender Dear"
"I Can't Give You Anything but Love"

A Nino Tempo—April Stevens Program—**RCA Camden CAS 824 (Nino Tempo is featured on Side 1, April on Side 2)**

Track Listing:
"Gimme a Little Kiss, Will Ya, Huh?"
"The Tricks of the Trade"

"I'm in Love Again"
"Put Me in Your Pocket"
"Dreamy Melody"

1966
***Hey Baby!* (With Nino Tempo)—Atco 33-180 (Mono) and Atco SD 33-180 (Stereo)**

Track Listing:
"Swing Me"
"Hey Baby! "
"Land of 1,000 Dances"
"No Hair Sam" (April Solo)
"Poison of Your Kiss"
"Ooh La La"
"I Love How You Love Me" (With Nino and the Guilloteenes)
"These Arms of Mine"
"Teach Me Tiger" (1965) (April Solo)
"The Coldest Night of the Year"
"Tomorrow Is Soon a Memory"
"Think of You"

***All Strung Out* (With Nino Tempo)—White Whale WW-113 (Mono) and White Whale WW-7113 (Stereo)**

Track Listing:
"You'll Be Needing Me Baby"
"Help You to See"
"All Strung Out"
"Follow Me"
"Little Child"
"Alone Alone"
"Sunny" (April Solo)

"Out of Nowhere"
"Wings of Love"
"I Can't Go On Living Baby Without You"
"Bye Bye Blues"
"The Habit of Lovin' You Baby"

1973
Love Story and Their Hits of Yesterday, Today & Tomorrow **(With Nino Tempo)—A&M 87 980 IT (Released only in the Netherlands)**

Track Listing:
"Love Story"
"Who Turns Me On"
"Sweet and Lovely" (Re-Recording)
"Put It Where You Want It"
"I Can't Get Over You Baby"
"Deep Purple" (Re-Recording)
"All Strung Out" (Re-Recording)
"Whispering" (Re-Recording)
"I Can't Go On Living Baby Without You" (Re-Recording)
"Gotta Leave You Baby" (April Solo)

1982
Deep Purple (With Nino Tempo)—Arrival 8151 (Released Only In The Netherlands)

Track Listing:
"Deep Purple" (Re-Recording)
"Whispering" (Re-Recording)
"Jackson"
"When" (Nino Solo)
"You Don't Have to Be a Star (To Be In My Show) "

"I Got You Babe"
"If You Go"
"Love Will Keep Us Together" (April Solo)
"Love Story" (Re-Recording)
"You Turn Me On" (Re-Recording)
"A Little Too Much Love Was Not Enough" (Nino Solo)
"Little Man"
"I'm Leaving It All Up to You"
"Swinging on a Star"
"To Know You Is to Love You"
"Don't Go Breaking My Heart"

1985
Alone—Mr. Sam 1/Palace PLM S6541

Track Listing:
"Alone"
"Once Upon a Very Special Time"
"I Understand"
"Lovers and Other Strangers"
"With You I'm Born Again/Could It Be Magic"
"To Sleep Perchance to Dream"
"How Did He Look"
"Carousel Dreams"

DISCOGRAPHY SINGLE RELEASES

1990
***Carousel Dreams*—USA Music Group USACD-635**

Track Listing:
"I Understand"
"I Remember (Recuerdo)"
"Carousel Dreams"
"Once Upon a Very Special Time"
"How Did He Look"
"I Never Loved Anyone Like I Love You"
"Alone"
"With You I'm Born Again/Could It Be Magic"
"To Sleep Perchance to Dream"
"Please Be Gentle"
"I Remember (Recuerdo)"—Foreign Release Only

1995
***Sweet and Lovely*—*The Best of Nino Tempo & April* Stevens (With Nino Tempo)—Varese Sarabande VSD-5592**

Track Listing:
"Deep Purple"
"Sweet and Lovely"
"Teach Me Tiger" (April Solo)
"Paradise"
"(We'll Always Be) Together"
"Begin the Beguine"

"Whispering"
"Stardust"
"Tea for Two"
"I'm Confessin' That I Love You"
"The Coldest Night of the Year"
"I Love How You Love Me"
"All Strung Out"
"You'll Be Needing Me Baby"
"I Can't Go On Livin' Baby Without You"
"I'm Fallin' For You"
"What Don't You Do Right?"

1999
***All Strung Out* (With Nino Tempo)—Varese Sarabande VSD 6036**

Track Listing same as LP PLUS:
"My Old Flame"
"Let It Be Me"
"Ooh Poo Pa Doo"
"Please Help Me I'm Falling"

2001
***Deep Purple/Nino and April Sing the Great Songs* (With Nino Tempo) (Two LPs on One CD)—Collectables COL-CD6888**

Track Listing Same as LPs

2008
***Teach Me Tiger*—Harkit HRKCD 8291**

Track Listing same as LP PLUS:
"That Warm Afternoon"

"Aw, C'mon"
"Jonny"
"You and Only You"
"Love Kitten"
"Gimme a Little Kiss, Will Ya, Huh? "
"The Tricks of the Trade"
"I'm in Love Again (Original RCA Version)"
"Put Me in Your Pocket"
"Dreamy Melody"

2010
***Hey Baby!* (With Nino Tempo—Tartare T-8003 (Collector's Choice Music ccmusic.com)**

Track Listing Same as LP

2011
***Hey, Baby! The Nino Tempo & April Stevens Anthology* (With Nino Tempo)—Ace CDCHD 1301**

Track Listing:
"Deep Purple"
"All Strung Out"
"Sweet and Lovely"
"Wanting You" (April Solo)
"You'll Be Needing Me Baby"
"Honeysuckle Rose"
"I Love How You Love Me"
"Follow Me"
"Whispering"
"Hey Baby"
"Love Kitten" (April Solo)
"The Habit of Lovin' You Baby"

"The Coldest Night of the Year"
"Alone Alone"
"Lovin' Valentine" (April Solo)
"Out of Nowhere"
"Wings of Love"
"Teach Me Tiger" (April Solo)
"Boys' Town (Where My Broken Hearted Buddies Go)" (Nino Solo)
"I Can't Go On Livin' Baby Without You"
"Sister James" (Nino Tempo & (5th Ave Sax)
"Amazon River" (Nino Tempo)
"Soft Warm Lips" (April Solo)
"America's Weather Girl" (April's 1966 Radio Spots)

2013
No, No, No! Not That!—Harkit HRKCD 8422

Track Listing:
"No, No, No! Not That! "
"Black Lace"
"Don't Do It"
"Shadow Waltz"
"Later Perhaps, Not Now"
"I Love the Way You're Breaking My Heart"
"Meant to Tell You"
"My Lost Melody"
"Why Can't a Boy and Girl Just Stay In Love?"
"That Naughty Waltz"
"Sabor a Mi"
"The Sweetest Day"
"Morning 'Til Midnight"
"Wanting You"
"Falling In Love Again"

"The Story of Love"
"How Could Red Riding Hood (Have Been So Very Good)"
"You Said You'd Do It (Are You Gonna?)"
"Hot Tamale"
"Treat Me Nice"
"Soft Warm Lips"
"C'est Si Bon"
"I Like to Talk to Myself"

Made in United States
Orlando, FL
10 February 2024